HOUGHTON MIFFLIN

MATH
Expressions
Common Core

Dr. Karen C. Fuson

GRADE

4

This material is based upon work supported by the
National Science Foundation
under Grant Numbers
ESI-9816320, REC-9806020, and RED-935373.

Any opinions, findings, and conclusions, or recommendations expressed in this material
are those of the author and do not necessarily reflect the views of the National Science Foundation.

HOUGHTON MIFFLIN HARCOURT

CONTENTS

© Houghton Mifflin Harcourt Publishing Company

CONTENTS (continued)

Dear Family,

Your child is learning math in an innovative program called *Math Expressions*. In Unit 1, your child will use place value drawings and charts to understand that the value of each place is 10 times greater than the value of the place to its right. This understanding is essential when comparing, rounding, or adding multidigit numbers. *Math Expressions* encourages children to think about "making new groups" to help them understand place values.

We call the method below "New Groups Above". The numbers that represent the new groups are written above the problem.

1. Add the ones:

5 + 7 = 12 ones
12 = 2 ones + 10 ones,
and 10 ones = 1 new ten.

$$\begin{array}{r} \overset{1}{5,1\,7\,5} \\ +\,3,9\,6\,7 \\ \hline 2 \end{array}$$

2. Add the tens:

1 + 7 + 6 = 14 tens
14 = 4 tens + 10 tens,
and 10 tens = 1 new hundred.

$$\begin{array}{r} \overset{1\ 1}{5,1\,7\,5} \\ +\,3,9\,6\,7 \\ \hline 4\ 2 \end{array}$$

3. Add the hundreds:

1 + 1 + 9 = 11 hundreds
11 = 1 hundred + 10 hundreds,
and 10 hundreds = 1 new thousand.

$$\begin{array}{r} \overset{1\ \ 1\ 1}{5,1\,7\,5} \\ +\,3,9\,6\,7 \\ \hline 1\ 4\ 2 \end{array}$$

4. Add the thousands:

1 + 5 + 3 = 9 thousands

$$\begin{array}{r} \overset{1\ \ 1\ 1}{5,1\,7\,5} \\ +\,3,9\,6\,7 \\ \hline 9,1\,4\,2 \end{array}$$

We call the following method "New Groups Below." The steps are the same, but the new groups are written below the addends.

It is easier to see the totals for each column (12 and 14) and adding is easier because you add the two numbers you see and then add the 1.

1.
$$\begin{array}{r} 5,1\,7\,5 \\ +\,3,9\,6\,7 \\ \hline {\scriptstyle 1}\ 2 \end{array}$$

2.
$$\begin{array}{r} 5,1\,7\,5 \\ +\,3,9\,6\,7 \\ \hline {\scriptstyle 1\,1}\ \ \\ 4\ 2 \end{array}$$

3.
$$\begin{array}{r} 5,1\,7\,5 \\ +\,3,9\,6\,7 \\ \hline {\scriptstyle 1\,1\,1} \\ 1\ 4\ 2 \end{array}$$

4.
$$\begin{array}{r} 5,1\,7\,5 \\ +\,3,9\,6\,7 \\ \hline {\scriptstyle 1\,1\,1} \\ 9,1\,4\,2 \end{array}$$

It is important that your child maintains his or her home practice with basic multiplication and division.

Sincerely,
Your child's teacher

COMMON CORE This unit includes the Common Core Standards for Mathematical Content for Number and Operations in Base Ten and Measurement and Data, 4.NBT.1, 4.NBT.2, 4.NBT.3, 4.NBT.4, 4.MD.2 and all Mathematical Practices.

Estimada familia,

Su niño está aprendiendo matemáticas mediante el programa *Math Expressions*. En la Unidad 1, se usarán dibujos y tablas de valor posicional para comprender que el valor de cada lugar es 10 veces mayor que el valor del lugar a su derecha. Comprender esto es esencial para comparar, redondear o sumar números de varios dígitos. *Math Expressions* enseña a pensar en "formar grupos nuevos" para comprender los valores posicionales.

Este método se llama "Grupos nuevos arriba". Los números que representan los grupos nuevos se escriben arriba del problema:

1. Suma las unidades:

$5 + 7 = 12$ unidades
$12 = 2$ unidades $+ 10$ unidades,
y 10 unidades $= 1$ nueva decena.

$$\begin{array}{r} \overset{1}{5,1}\overset{}{7}5 \\ + 3,967 \\ \hline 2 \end{array}$$

2. Suma las decenas:

$1 + 7 + 6 = 14$ decenas
$14 = 4$ decenas $+ 10$ decenas,
y 10 decenas $= 1$ nueva centena.

$$\begin{array}{r} \overset{1\ 1}{5,1}7 5 \\ + 3,967 \\ \hline 4\,2 \end{array}$$

3. Suma las centenas:

$1 + 1 + 9 = 11$ centenas
$11 = 1$ centenas $+ 10$ centenas,
y 10 centenas $= 1$ nuevo millar.

$$\begin{array}{r} \overset{1\ 1\ 1}{5,1}7 5 \\ + 3,967 \\ \hline 1\,4\,2 \end{array}$$

4. Suma los millares:

$1 + 5 + 3 = 9$ millares

$$\begin{array}{r} \overset{1\ 1\ 1}{5,1}7 5 \\ + 3,967 \\ \hline 9,1\,4\,2 \end{array}$$

Este método se llama "Grupos nuevos abajo". Los pasos son iguales, pero los nuevos grupos se escriben abajo de los sumandos:

Es más fácil ver los totales de cada columna (12 y 14) y es más fácil sumar porque sumas los dos números que ves, y luego sumas 1.

1.
$$\begin{array}{r} 5,175 \\ + 3,967 \\ \hline 1 \\ 2 \end{array}$$

2.
$$\begin{array}{r} 5,175 \\ + 3,967 \\ \hline 1\ 1 \\ 4\,2 \end{array}$$

3.
$$\begin{array}{r} 5,175 \\ + 3,967 \\ \hline 1\ 1\ 1 \\ 1\,4\,2 \end{array}$$

4.
$$\begin{array}{r} 5,175 \\ + 3,967 \\ \hline 1\ 1\ 1 \\ 9,1\,4\,2 \end{array}$$

Es importante que su niño siga practicando las multiplicaciones y divisiones básicas en casa.

Atentamente,
El maestro de su niño

COMMON CORE

Esta unidad incluye los Common Core Standards for Mathematical Content for Number and Operations in Base Ten and Measurement and Data, 4.NBT.1, 4.NBT.2, 4.NBT.3, 4.NBT.4, 4.MD.2 and all Mathematical Practices.

Dear Family,

In this unit, your child will be learning about the common multiplication method that most adults know. However, they will also explore ways to draw multiplication. *Math Expressions* uses area of rectangles to show multiplication.

	30	+	7
20	$20 \times 30 = 600$		$20 \times 7 = 140$
+			
4	$4 \times 30 = 120$		$4 \times 7 = 28$

Area Method:

$20 \times 30 = 600$
$20 \times 7 = 140$
$4 \times 30 = 120$
$4 \times 7 = \ \ 28$
Total $= 888$

Shortcut Method:

$\overset{1}{\underset{2}{\ }}$
37
$\times\ 24$
148
74
888

Area drawings help all students see multiplication. They also help students remember what numbers they need to multiply and what numbers make up the total.

Your child will also learn to find products involving single-digit numbers, tens, and hundreds by factoring the tens or hundreds. For example,

$$200 \times 30 = 2 \times 100 \times 3 \times 10$$
$$= 2 \times 3 \times 100 \times 10$$
$$= 6 \times 1,000 = 6,000$$

By observing the zeros patterns in products like these, your child will learn to do such multiplications mentally.

If your child is still not confident with single-digit multiplication and division, we urge you to set aside a few minutes every night for multiplication and division practice. In a few more weeks, the class will be doing multidigit division, so it is very important that your child be both fast and accurate with basic multiplication and division.

If you need practice materials, please contact me.

Sincerely,
Your child's teacher

COMMON CORE   This unit includes the Common Core Standards for Mathematical Content for Operations and Algebraic Thinking, Number and Operations in Base Ten and Measurement and Data, 4.OA.3, 4.NBT.1, 4.NBT.2, 4.NBT.3, 4.NBT.5, 4.MD.2 and all Mathematical Practices.

Estimada familia:

En esta unidad, su niño estará aprendiendo el método de multiplicación común que la mayoría de los adultos conoce. Sin embargo, también explorará maneras de dibujar la multiplicación. Para mostrar la multiplicación, *Math Expressions* usa el método del área del rectángulo.

	30	+	7
20	20 × 30 = 600		20 × 7 = 140
+			
4	4 × 30 = 120		4 × 7 = 28

Método del área

$20 \times 30 = 600$
$20 \times 7 = 140$
$4 \times 30 = 120$
$4 \times 7 = 28$
Total $= 888$

Método más corto

$$\begin{array}{r} \overset{1}{}\overset{2}{} \\ 37 \\ \times\ 24 \\ \hline 148 \\ 74 \\ \hline 888 \end{array}$$

Los dibujos de área ayudan a los estudiantes a visualizar la multiplicación. También los ayuda a recordar cuáles números tienen que multiplicar y cuáles números forman el total.

Su niño también aprenderá a hallar productos relacionados con números de un solo dígito, con decenas y con centenas, factorizando las decenas o las centenas. Por ejemplo:

$200 \times 30 = 2 \times 100 \times 3 \times 10$
$ = 2 \times 3 \times 100 \times 10$
$ = 6 \times 1{,}000 = 6{,}000$

Al observar los patrones de ceros en productos como estos, su niño aprenderá a hacer dichas multiplicaciones mentalmente.

Si su niño todavía no domina la multiplicación y la división con números de un solo dígito, le sugerimos que dedique algunos minutos todas las noches para practicar la multiplicación y la división. Dentro de pocas semanas, la clase hará divisiones con números de varios dígitos, por eso es muy importante que su niño haga las operaciones básicas de multiplicación y de división de manera rápida y exacta.

Si necesita materiales para practicar, comuníquese conmigo.

Atentamente,
El maestro de su niño

Esta unidad incluye los Common Core Standards for Mathematical Content for Operations and Algebraic Thinking, Number and Operations in Base Ten and Measurement and Data, 4.OA.3, 4.NBT.1, 4.NBT.2, 4.NBT.3, 4.NBT.5, 4.MD.2 and all Mathematical Practices.

Arrays and Area Models

▶ Model a Product of Tens

Olivia wants to tile the top of a table. The table is 20 inches by 30 inches. Olivia needs to find the area of the table in inches.

2. Find the area of this 20 × 30 rectangle by dividing it into 10-by-10 squares of 100.

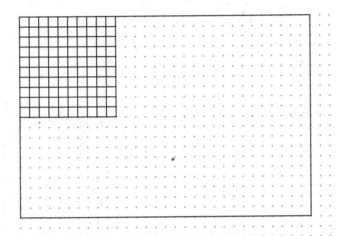

3. Each tile is a 1-inch square. How many tiles does Olivia need to cover the tabletop? _____

4. Each box of tiles contains 100 tiles. How many boxes of tiles does Olivia need to buy? _____

▶ Factor the Tens

5. Complete the steps to show your work in Exercise 2 numerically.

$20 × 30 = ($ _____ $× 10) × ($ _____ $× 10)$

$= ($ _____ $×$ _____ $) × (10 × 10)$

$=$ _____ $×100$

$= 600$

6. Is it true that 20 × 30 = 30 × 20? Explain how you know.

_____

_____

VOCABULARY
factor
product

▶ Look for Patterns

Multiplying greater numbers in your head is easier when you learn patterns of multiplication with tens.

Start with column A and look for the patterns used to get the expressions in each column. Copy and complete the table.

Table 1

	A	B	C	D
	2 × 3	2 × 1 × 3 × 1	6 × 1	6
1.	2 × 30	2 × 1 × 3 × 10	6 × 10	_____
2.	20 × 30	2 × 10 × 3 × 10	_____	_____

3. How are the expressions in column B different from the expressions in column A?

_____

_____

_____

4. In column C, we see that each expression can be written as a number times a place value. Which of these **factors** gives more information about the size of the **product?**

_____

5. Why is 6 the first digit of the products in column D?

_____

6. Why are there different numbers of zeros in the products in column D?

_____

_____

▶ Compare Tables

Copy and complete each table.

Table 2

	A	B	C	D
	6×3	$6 \times 1 \times 3 \times 1$	18×1	18
7.	6×30	$6 \times 1 \times 3 \times 10$	18×10	_____
8.	60×30	$6 \times 10 \times 3 \times 10$	_____	_____

Table 3

	A	B	C	D
	5×8	$5 \times 1 \times 8 \times 1$	40×1	40
9.	5×80	$5 \times 1 \times 8 \times 10$	40×10	_____
10.	50×80	_____	_____	_____

11. Why do the products in Table 2 have more digits than the products in Table 1?

_____

_____

12. Why are there more zeros in the products in Table 3 than the products in Table 2?

_____

_____

▶ Explore the Area Model

1. How many square units of area are there in the tens part of the drawing? _____

2. What multiplication equation gives the area of the tens part of the drawing? Write this equation in its rectangle.

   _____

3. How many square units of area are there in the ones part? _____

4. What multiplication equation gives the area of the ones part? Write this equation in its rectangle. _____

5. What is the total of the two areas? _____

6. How do you know that 104 is the correct product of 4×26?

   _____

7. Read problems A and B.
   A. Al's photo album has 26 pages. Each page has 4 photos. How many photos are in Al's album?

   B. Nick took 4 photos. Henri took 26 photos. How many more photos did Henri take than Nick?

   Which problem could you solve using the multiplication you just did? Explain why.

   _____

   _____

   _____

Model One-Digit by Two-Digit Multiplication

▶ Use the Place Value Sections Method

You can use an area model to demonstrate the
Place Value Sections Method. This strategy is
used below for multiplying a one-digit number
by a two-digit number.

Complete the steps.

27 =	20	+ 7	
5	5 × 20 = 100	5 × 7 = 35	5

+ ___
___

**Use the Place Value Sections Method to solve the problem.
Complete the steps.**

1. The fourth-grade class is participating in a walk-a-thon.
   Each student will walk 8 laps around the track. There
   are 92 fourth-grade students. How many laps will the
   fourth-grade class walk?

   _____

92 =	90	+	2	
8	___ × ___ = ___		___ × ___ = ___	8

+ ___
___

**Draw an area model and use the Place Value Sections
Method to solve the problem.**

2. A football coach is ordering 3 shirts for each football player.
   There are 54 players in the football program. How many
   shirts does the coach need to order for the entire program?

   _____

▶ Use the Expanded Notation Method

You can also use an area model to show how to use the **Expanded Notation Method**. Use the Expanded Notation Method to solve 5×27 below.

Complete the steps.

3.

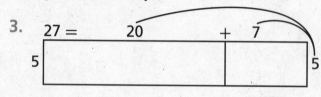

$$27 = \underline{\quad} + \underline{\quad}$$
$$\times 5 = \underline{\quad}$$
$$\underline{\quad} \times \underline{\quad} = \underline{\quad}$$
$$\underline{\quad} \times \underline{\quad} = \underline{\quad}$$
$$\underline{\quad}$$

Use the Expanded Notation Method to solve the problem. Complete the steps.

4. A farm stand sold 4 bushels of apples in one day. Each bushel of apples weighs 42 pounds. How many pounds of apples did the farm stand sell?

_____

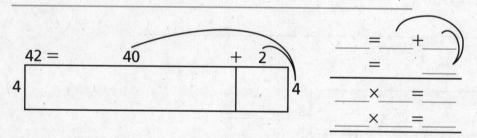

$$\underline{\quad} = \underline{\quad} + \underline{\quad}$$
$$\underline{\quad} = \underline{\quad}$$
$$\underline{\quad} \times \underline{\quad} = \underline{\quad}$$
$$\underline{\quad} \times \underline{\quad} = \underline{\quad}$$
$$\underline{\quad}$$

Draw an area model and use the Expanded Notation Method to solve the problem.

5. A marina needs to replace the boards on their pier. The pier is 7 feet by 39 feet. What is the area of the boards that need to be replaced?

_____

▶ Use the Algebraic Notation Method to Multiply

Another numerical multiplication method that can be represented by an area model is the **Algebraic Notation Method**. This method also decomposes the two-digit factor into tens and ones and then uses the Distributive Property.

Use the Algebraic Notation Method to solve each problem. Complete the steps.

4. $8 \cdot 62$

$62 = $ _____ $+$ _____

_____

$$8 \cdot 62 = \underline{} \cdot (\underline{} + \underline{})$$
$$= 480 + 16$$
$$= 496$$

5. $2 \cdot 97$

$97 = $ _____ $+$ _____

_____

$$2 \cdot 97 = \underline{} \cdot (\underline{} + \underline{})$$
$$= 180 + 14$$
$$= 194$$

Draw an area model and use the Algebraic Notation Method to solve the problem.

6. There are 9 members on the school's golf team. Each golfer hit a bucket of 68 golf balls at the driving range. How many golf balls did the entire team hit?

_____

7. What is the first step in the Algebraic Notation Method?

_____

2-8 Class Activity

Name _____ **Date** _____

▶ Practice Different Methods.

Fill in the blanks in the following solutions.

3. 4 × 86

Expanded Notation

$$86 = \underline{\quad} + 6$$

$$\times \ 4 = \qquad \underline{\quad}$$

$$4 \times \underline{\quad} = \underline{\quad}$$

$$\underline{\quad} \times 6 = 24$$

$$\underline{\quad}$$

Algebraic Notation

$$4 \cdot 86 = \underline{\quad} \cdot (80 + 6)$$

$$= 320 + \underline{\quad}$$

$$= \underline{\quad}$$

4. 4 × 68

Expanded Notation

$$\underline{\quad} = 60 + 8$$

$$\times \ 4 = \qquad \underline{\quad}$$

$$4 \times \underline{\quad} = \underline{\quad}$$

$$\underline{\quad} \times 8 = 32$$

$$\underline{\quad}$$

Algebraic Notation

$$4 \cdot 68 = 4 \cdot (\underline{\quad} + \underline{\quad})$$

$$= 240 + \underline{\quad}$$

$$= \underline{\quad}$$

Solve using a numerical method. Draw the related area model.

5. 5 × 64 = _____

6. 6 × 72 = _____

7. 7 × 92 = _____

8. 8 × 53 = _____

9. 5 × 46 = _____

10. 6 × 27 = _____

Houghton Mifflin Harcourt Publishing Company

Compare Methods of One-Digit by Two-Digit Multiplication

VOCABULARY
Distributive Property
estimate
partial products
rounding

▶ Vocabulary

Choose the best term from the box.

1. _____ are the products of the ones, tens, hundreds, and so on in multidigit multiplication. **(Lessons 2-7)**

2. An _____ is a number close to an exact amount. **(Lesson 2-5)**

3. The _____ lets you find a number times a sum by multiplying the number by each addend and then adding the products. **(Lessons 2-7)**

▶ Concepts and Skills

4. Write the steps for finding 50×30 by factoring the tens. **(Lesson 2-2)**

_____

_____

5. Explain how you know that $10 \times 60 = 600$. **(Lesson 2-2)**

_____

_____

6. Explain how the Expanded Notation Method is similar to the Place Value Sections Method when multiplying a one-digit number by a two-digit number. **(Lesson 2-6)**

_____

_____

7. Use mental math to find each product. **(Lesson 2-3)**

4×7 _____ 4×700 _____

4×70 _____ $4 \times 7,000$ _____

40×70 _____

Multiply using any method. Show your work.
(Lessons 2-8, 2-10, 2-14)

8. 3×68 _____

9. 5×84 _____

10. 3×506 _____

11. 9×265 _____

12. 16×50 _____

13. 12×32 _____

14. $6 \times 4,518$ _____

15. $4 \times 2,706$ _____

Estimate each product. Solve to check your estimate.
(Lessons 2-5, 2-14, 2-17)

16. 7×82

_____

_____

_____

17. 33×66

_____

_____

_____

18. 46×20

_____

_____

_____

19. $9 \times 3,276$

_____

_____

_____

▶ Problem Solving

Find the exact cost. (Lessons 2-4, 2-10)

20. A rental car costs $63 per day. If someone rents the car for 6 days, how much will be the total cost?

_____

21. The Adventure Club is going skating. The price of admission to the skating rink is $3 per person. If there are 214 people in the club, how much will it cost the club to skate?

_____

22. A travel agent is booking flights for a group of 9 people. If each airplane ticket costs $184, how much will their tickets cost altogether?

_____

Solve each problem. List any extra numerical information. *show your work.*
(Lesson 2-15)

23. Mariah is painting wall murals in the cafeteria. One mural is 12 feet by 28 feet. The other mural is 12 feet by 32 feet. What is the total area of the cafeteria that Mariah is painting?

_____

24. A family spent 7 hours at the zoo. They bought 2 adult tickets for $20 each and 3 child tickets for $10 each. They bought lunch for $23. How much did the tickets cost?

_____

25. **Extended Response** Sketch an area model for the product $6 \times 3{,}243$. Explain how the area model can be used to find the product. **(Lesson 2-16)**

_____

_____

_____

_____

_____

_____

Dear Family,

Your child is familiar with multiplication from earlier units. Unit 3 of *Math Expressions* extends the concepts used in multiplication to teach your child division. The main goals of this unit are to:

• Learn methods for dividing whole numbers up to four digits.

• Use estimates to check the reasonableness of answers.

• Solve problems involving division and remainders.

Your child will learn and practice techniques such as the Place Value Sections, Expanded Notation, and Digit-by-Digit methods to gain speed and accuracy in division. At first, your child will learn to use patterns and multiplication to divide. Later, your child will learn to use the methods with divisors from 2 to 9. Then your child will learn to divide when there is a zero in the quotient or dividend and to watch out for potential problems involving these situations.

Examples of Division Methods:

Your child may use whatever method he or she chooses as long as he or she can explain it. Some children like to use different methods.

Place Value Sections Method	Expanded Notation Method	Digit-by-Digit Method

Place Value Sections Method:

$$60 + 6 = 66$$

$$5 \overline{\begin{array}{c|c} 330 & 30 \\ -300 & 30 \\ \hline 30 & 0 \end{array}}$$

Expanded Notation Method:

$$\begin{array}{r} 6 \\ 60 \\ 5\overline{)330} \\ -300 \\ \hline 30 \\ -30 \\ \hline 0 \end{array} \Big] 66$$

Digit-by-Digit Method:

$$\begin{array}{r} 66 \\ 5\overline{)330} \\ -30 \\ \hline 30 \\ -30 \\ \hline 0 \end{array}$$

Your child will also learn to interpret remainders in the context of the problem being solved; for example, when the remainder alone is the answer to a word problem.

Finally, your child will apply this knowledge to solve mixed problems with one or more steps and using all four operations.

If you have questions or problems, please contact me.

Sincerely,
Your child's teacher

COMMON CORE This unit includes the Common Core Standards for Mathematical Content for Numbers and Operations in Base Ten, 4.NBT.6 and all Mathematical Practices.

Estimada familia:

En unidades anteriores su niño se ha familiarizado con la multiplicación. La Unidad 3 de *Math Expressions* amplía los conceptos usados en la multiplicación para que su niño aprenda la división. Los objetivos principales de esta unidad son:

• aprender métodos para dividir números enteros de hasta cuatro dígitos.

• usar la estimación para comprobar si las respuestas son razonables.

• resolver problemas que requieran división y residuos.

Su niño aprenderá y practicará técnicas tales como las de Secciones de valor posicional, Notación extendida y Dígito por dígito, para adquirir rapidez y precisión en la división. Al principio, su niño aprenderá a usar patrones y la multiplicación para dividir. Más adelante, usará los métodos con divisores de 2 a 9. Luego, aprenderá a dividir cuando haya un cero en el cociente o en el dividendo, y a detectar problemas que pueden surgir en esas situaciones.

Ejemplos de métodos de división:

Secciones de valor posicional	Notación extendida	Dígito por dígito

$$
\begin{array}{r}
60 + \quad 6 = 66 \\
5\overline{\begin{array}{|c|c|}
\hline
330 & 30 \\
-300 & 30 \\
\hline
30 & 0 \\
\end{array}}
\end{array}
\qquad
\begin{array}{r}
6 \\
60 \, \big] 66 \\
5\overline{)330} \\
-300 \\
\hline
30 \\
-30 \\
\hline
0
\end{array}
\qquad
\begin{array}{r}
66 \\
5\overline{)330} \\
-30 \\
\hline
30 \\
-30 \\
\hline
0
\end{array}
$$

Su niño puede usar el método que elija siempre y cuando pueda explicarlo. A algunos niños les gusta usar métodos diferentes.

Su niño también aprenderá a interpretar los residuos en el contexto del problema que se esté resolviendo; por ejemplo, cuando solamente el residuo es la respuesta a un problema.

Por último, su niño aplicará este conocimiento para resolver problemas mixtos de uno o más pasos, usando las cuatro operaciones.

Si tiene alguna pregunta o comentario, por favor comuníquese conmigo.

Atentamente,
El maestro de su niño

© Houghton Mifflin Harcourt Publishing Company

COMMON CORE Esta unidad incluye los Common Core Standards for Mathematical Content for Numbers and Operations in Base Ten, 4.NBT.6 and all Mathematical Practices.

Divide With Remainders

▶ Divide with Remainders

**The remainder must be less than the divisor.
If it is not, increase the quotient.**

```
       3                    4 R3
    5)23                 5)23
    −15                  −20
    ─────                ─────
      8 no                 3 yes
        8 > 5                3 < 5
```
⟶

```
       8                    9 R6
    9)87                 9)87
    −72                  −81
    ─────                ─────
     15 no                 6 yes
       15 > 9               6 < 9
```
⟶

Divide with remainders.

1. 2)19

2. 7)50

3. 9)48

4. 5)48

5. 6)19

6. 3)25

Divide. Multiply to check the last problem in each row.

7. 6)27

8. 4)30

9.
```
       5 R4
    7)39
    − 35
    ─────
       4
```

$7 \cdot 5 + 4 =$
$35 + 4 = 39$

10. 8)43

11. 5)26

12. 9)41

13. 5)32

14. 4)21

15. 3)22

► Multiplying and Dividing

Complete the steps.

1. Sam divides 738 by 6. He uses the Place Value
   Sections Method and the Expanded Notation Method.

   a. Sam thinks: I'll draw the Place Value Sections that I know from
      multiplication. To divide, I need to find how many hundreds,
      tens, and ones to find the unknown factor.

   Place Value Sections Method   **Expanded Notation Method**

   __hundreds + __tens + __ones $6\overline{)738}$
   __00   __0   __

6	738		

   b. 6 × 100 = 600 will fit. 6 × 200 = 1,200 is too big.

   __00   +   _0   +   _ $6\overline{)738}$

6	738		

   c. I have 138 left for the other sections.
      6 × 20 = 120 will fit. 6 × 30 = 180 is too big.

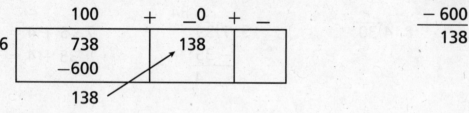

$$\begin{array}{r} 100 \\ 6\overline{)738} \\ -600 \\ \hline 138 \end{array}$$

   d. 6 × 3 = 18

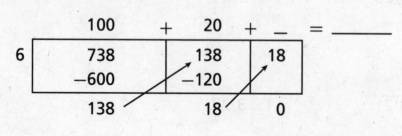

$$\begin{array}{r} 20 \\ 100 \\ 6\overline{)738} \\ -600 \\ \hline 138 \\ -120 \\ \hline 18 \end{array}$$

▶ Practice the Place Value Sections Method

Solve. Use Place Value Sections Method for division.

1. The sidewalk crew knows that the new sidewalk at the mall will be 3,915 square feet. It will be 9 feet wide. How long will it be? _____

$$\underline{400} + \underline{30} + \underline{5} = 435$$

	400	30	5
9 ft	3,915 −3,600	315 −270	45 −45
	315	45	0

2. The sidewalk at the theater will be 2,748 square feet. It will be 6 feet wide. How long will it be?

_____

$$\underline{}00 + \underline{}0 + \underline{} = \underline{}$$

3. Pens are packaged in boxes of 8. The store is charged for a total of 4,576 pens. How many boxes of pens did they receive? _____

$$\underline{}00 + \underline{}0 + \underline{} = \underline{}$$

4. A factory has 2,160 erasers. They package them in groups of 5. How many packages of erasers does the factory have? _____

$$\underline{} + \underline{} + \underline{} = \underline{}$$

5. A party planner has 834 small flowers to make party favors. She will put 3 flowers in each party favor. How many party favors can she make? _____

$$\underline{} + \underline{} + \underline{} = \underline{}$$

6. An artist has 956 tiles to use in a design. He plans to arrange the tiles in group of 4 tiles. How many groups of 4 tiles can he make?

_____

$$\underline{} + \underline{} + \underline{} = \underline{}$$

Name _____ **Date** _____

▶ 2-Digit and 4-Digit Quotients

Solve. Use the Place Value Sections and the Expanded Notation Methods for division.

1.

$$20 + 8 = 28$$

9	252	72
	− 180	− 72
	72	0

$9\overline{)252}$

2.

$$\underline{}0 + \underline{} = \underline{}$$

6	162	

$6\overline{)162}$

3.

$$\underline{},000 + \underline{}00 + \underline{}0 + \underline{} = \underline{}$$

8	8,984			

$8\overline{)8,984}$

4.

$$\underline{},000 + \underline{}00 + \underline{}0 + \underline{} = \underline{}$$

3	7,722			

$3\overline{)7,722}$

Discuss 2-Digit and 4-Digit Quotients

Name _____   Date _____

▶ Practice

Divide.

6. 4)868

7. 6)5,142

8. 3)4,395

9. 4)332

10. 7)1,617

11. 7)939

12. 2)4,276

13. 6)2,576

14. 7)441

15. 9)3,735

16. 7)406

17. 3)9,954

Name _____ Date _____

► Practice

Divide.

6. $5\overline{)965}$

7. $8\overline{)128}$

8. $8\overline{)928}$

9. $3\overline{)716}$

10. $4\overline{)4,596}$

11. $4\overline{)982}$

12. $3\overline{)6,342}$

13. $8\overline{)578}$

14. $5\overline{)1,155}$

15. $6\overline{)3,336}$

16. $7\overline{)672}$

17. $3\overline{)4,152}$

Digit-by-Digit Method

Name _____   Date _____

▶ Vocabulary

Choose the best term from the box.

1. A _____ is an answer to a division problem. (Lesson 3-1)

2. The number 7 is the _____ in the division problem 548 ÷ 7. (Lesson 3-1)

3. In the division problem 548 ÷ 7, the number 548 is the _____. (Lesson 3-1)

▶ Concepts and Skills

4. List the three methods suggested in this Unit for solving division problems. Which division method would you use to solve 728 ÷ 6? Explain why you chose that method and how you would use it to solve the problem. (Lessons 3-2, 3-3, 3-4, 3-5)

   _____

   _____

5. Explain why you need to write a zero in the tens place of the quotient when you divide 829 by 4. (Lesson 3-7)

   _____

   _____

   _____

6. For what types of real world division problems might you use the quotient alone? When might you use only the remainder? (Lesson 3-9)

   _____

   _____

Use rounding and estimation to decide whether each quotient makes sense. (Lesson 3-8)

7. $6\overline{)297}$ 49 R3

8. $4\overline{)3{,}256}$ 814

9. $8\overline{)4{,}229}$ 528 R5

Use any method to solve. (Lessons 3-1, 3-2, 3-3, 3-4, 3-5, 3-6, 3-7)

10. $4\overline{)716}$ 11. $9\overline{)959}$ 12. $3\overline{)6,243}$ 13. $7\overline{)940}$

14. $4\overline{)2,203}$ 15. $7\overline{)8,659}$ 16. $5\overline{)7,534}$ 17. $6\overline{)9,915}$

▶ Problem Solving

Solve.

18. There are 185 students going to a museum. Each van can hold 9 students. How many vans of 9 students will there be? How many students will ride in a van that is not full? Lesson 3-9

_____

19. Joshua pulls 52 loads of sand on his wagon to make a play area. He pulls 21 pounds of sand on each load. How many pounds of sand does Joshua use to make a play area? Lesson 3-10

_____

20. **Extended Response** Kayla and her father baked 256 banana nut muffins and 298 chocolate chip muffins to sell at their family restaurant. They plan to place the muffins in boxes that hold 6 muffins each. What is the greatest number of boxes that can be filled with muffins? Explain how you found your answer. Lessons 3-9, 3-10

_____

_____

_____

Dear Family,

In Unit 4 of Math Expressions, your child will apply the skills he or she has learned about operations with whole numbers while solving real world problems involving addition, subtraction, multiplication, and division.

Your child will simplify and evaluate expressions. Parentheses will be introduced to show which operation should be done first. The symbols "=" and "≠" will be used to show whether numbers and expressions are equal.

Other topics of study in this unit include situation and solution equations for addition and subtraction, as well as multiplication and division. Your child will use situation equations to represent real world problems and solution equations to solve the problems. This method of representing a problem is particularly helpful when the problems contain greater numbers and students cannot solve mentally.

Your child will also solve multiplication and addition comparison problems and compare these types of problems identifying what is the same or different.

Addition Comparison	Multiplication Comparison
Angela is 14 years old. She is 4 years older than Damarcus. How old is Damarcus?	Shawn colored 5 pages in a coloring book. Anja colored 4 times as many pages as Shawn colored. How many pages did Anja color?

Students learn that in the addition problem they are adding 4, while in the multiplication problem, they are multiplying by 4.

Your child will apply this knowledge to solve word problems using all four operations and involving one or more steps.

Finally, your child will find factor pairs for whole numbers and generate and analyze numerical and geometric patterns.

If you have any questions or comments, please call or write to me.

Sincerely,
Your child's teacher

COMMON CORE

This unit includes the Common Core Standards for Mathematical Content for Operations and Algebraic Thinking 4.OA.1, 4.OA.2, 4.OA.3, 4.OA.4, 4.OA.5, Number and Operations in Base Ten 4.NBT.4, 4.NBT.5, 4.NBT.6, Measurement and Data 4.MD.2, and all Mathematical Practices.

Estimada familia:

En la Unidad 4 de Math Expressions, su hijo aplicará las destrezas relacionadas con operaciones de números enteros que ha adquirido, resolviendo problemas cotidianos que involucran suma, resta, multiplicación y división.

Su hijo simplificará y evaluará expresiones. Se introducirán los paréntesis como una forma de mostrar cuál operación deberá completarse primero. Los signos "=" y "≠" se usarán para mostrar si los números o las expresiones son iguales o no.

Otros temas de estudio en esta unidad incluyen ecuaciones de situación y de solución para la suma y resta, así como para la multiplicación y división. Su hijo usará ecuaciones de situación para representar problemas de la vida cotidiana y ecuaciones de solución para resolver esos problemas. Este método para representar problemas es particularmente útil cuando los problemas involucran números grandes y los estudiantes no pueden resolverlos mentalmente.

Su hijo también resolverá problemas de comparación de multiplicación y suma, y comparará este tipo de problemas para identificar las semejanzas y diferencias.

Comparación de suma	Comparación de multiplicación
Ángela tiene 14 años. Ella es 4 años mayor que Damarcus. ¿Cuántos años tiene Damarcus?	Shawn coloreó 5 páginas de un libro. Ana coloreó 4 veces ese número de páginas. ¿Cuántas páginas coloreó Ana?

Los estudiantes aprenderán que en el problema de suma están sumando 4, mientras que en el problema de multiplicación, están multiplicando por 4.

Su hijo aplicará estos conocimientos para resolver problemas de uno o más pasos usando las cuatro operaciones.

Finalmente, su hijo hallará pares de factores para números enteros y generará y analizará patrones numéricos y geométricos.

Si tiene alguna pregunta por favor comuníquese conmigo.

Atentamente,
El maestro de su niño

© Houghton Mifflin Harcourt Publishing Company

Properties and Algebraic Notation

▶ Discuss Inverse Operations

When you add, you put two groups together. When you subtract, you find an unknown addend or take away one group from another. Addition and subtraction are inverse operations. They undo each other.

Addends are numbers that are added to make a sum. You can find two addends for a sum by breaking apart the number.

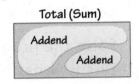

A break-apart drawing can help you find all eight related addition and subtraction equations for two addends.

Total (Sum)
81

72   9
Addend Addend

$81 = 72 + 9$ $72 + 9 = 81$

$81 = 9 + 72$ $9 + 72 = 81$

$72 = 81 - 9$ $81 - 9 = 72$

$9 = 81 - 72$ $81 - 72 = 9$

9. Which equations show the Commutative Property?

_____

10. What is the total in each equation? Where is the total in a subtraction equation?

_____

Solve each equation.

11. $50 = 30 + p$

    $p =$ _____

12. $q + 20 = 60$

    $q =$ _____

13. $90 - v = 50$

    $v =$ _____

14. Write the eight related addition and subtraction equations for the break-apart drawing.

56

48   8

_____   _____

_____   _____

_____   _____

_____   _____

© Houghton Mifflin Harcourt Publishing Company

▶ Discuss the Steps

1. Mr. Stills makes bags of school supplies for the 9 students in his class. He has 108 pencils and 72 erasers. He puts the same number of pencils and the same number of erasers into each bag. How many more pencils than erasers are in each bag of school supplies?

Solve the problem by finishing Nicole's and David's methods. Discuss what is alike and what is different about the methods.

Nicole's Method

Write an equation for each step.

Divide to find the number of pencils that Mr. Stills puts in each bag of school supplies.

$$108 \div 9 = \text{\_\_\_\_}$$

Divide to find the number of erasers that Mr. Stills puts in each bag of school supplies.

$$72 \div 9 = \text{\_\_\_\_}$$

Subtract the number of erasers in each bag from the number of pencils in each bag.

$$12 - 8 = \text{\_\_\_\_}$$

There are _____ more pencils than erasers in each bag of school supplies.

David's Method

Write an equation for the whole problem.

Let p = how many more pencils than erasers are in each bag of school supplies

The number of pencils in   The number of erasers in each
each bag of school supplies.   bag of school supplies.

$$\text{\_\_\_\_} \div 9 - \text{\_\_\_\_} \div 9 = p$$
$$12 - 8 = p$$
$$\text{\_\_\_\_} = p$$

There are _____ more pencils than erasers in each bag of school supplies.

Solve Multistep Problems

4-8

Class Activity

Name _____ Date _____

▶ Discuss the Steps (continued)

2. John is selling bags of popcorn for a school fundraiser. So far, John has sold 45 bags of popcorn for $5 each. His goal is to earn $300 for the school fundraiser. How many more bags of popcorn must John sell to reach his goal?

Solve the problem by writing an equation for each step. Then solve the problem by writing one equation for the whole problem.

Write an equation for each step.

Multiply to find how much money John has earned so far selling popcorn.

_____ × $5 = $_____

Subtract to find how much money John has left to earn to reach his goal.

$300 − $_____ = $_____

Divide to find the number of bags of popcorn John must sell to reach his goal.

$75 ÷ $5 = _____

John must sell _____ more bags of popcorn to reach his goal.

Write an equation for the whole problem.

Let b = the number of bags of popcorn John must sell to reach his goal.

John's fundraiser goal amount.   Amount of money John has raised so far.

(_____ − _____ × $5) ÷ $5 = b

($300 − $_____) ÷ $5 = b

$_____ ÷ $5 = b

_____ = b

John must sell _____ more bags of popcorn to reach his goal.

© Houghton Mifflin Harcourt Publishing Company

UNIT 4 LESSON 8

Solve Multistep Problems **41**

Name _____   Date _____

▶ Find Factor Pairs

A factor pair for a number is two whole numbers whose product is that number. For example, 2 and 5 is a factor pair for 10.

1. Draw arrays to show all the factor pairs for 12 on the grid below. The array for 1 and 12 is shown.

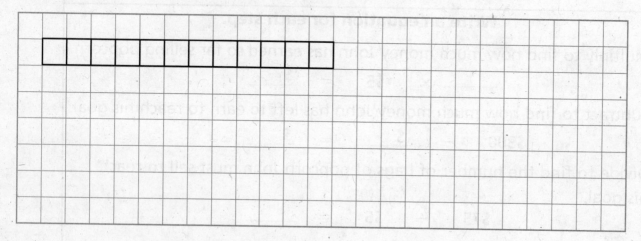

2. List all the factor pairs for 12. _____

Use the table to find all the factors pairs for each number.

3. 32

1	32
2	

4. 44

1	44

5. 100

1	100

List all the factor pairs for each number.

6. 29 _____

7. 63 _____

Factors and Prime Numbers

▶ Vocabulary

Choose the best term from the box.

1. A _____ shows the operation that can be used to solve a problem. (Lessons 4-2, 4-3)

2. A number greater than 1 that has 1 and itself as its only factor pair is a _____ (Lesson 4-10)

3. A _____ shows the structure of the information in a problem. (Lessons 4-2, 4-3)

▶ Concepts and Skills

4. Explain how the equation for *4 is 2 more than 2* is different from the equation for *4 is 2 times as many as 2*.
(Lessons 4-4, 4-5, 4-6)

_____

_____

_____

5. Explain how you could use rectangles and circles to show the following pattern: A B B A B B A B B. (Lesson 4-11)

_____

_____

6. Dori wrote this problem: Mrs. Ramos has 1,352 stamps. She buys some more stamps. Now she has 1,943 stamps. How many stamps did she buy? Explain why the situation equation $1,352 + s = 1,943$ represents Dori's problem. (Lesson 4-2)

_____

_____

_____

_____

Solve for ☐ or *n*. (Lesson 4-1)

7. $(18 - 9) \cdot 3 = \boxed{} \cdot 3$

   $\boxed{} = \underline{}$

8. $(35 + 50) - (25 \div 5) = n$

   $n = \underline{}$

List all factor pairs for each number. (Lesson 4-10)

9. 47

10. 28

Write whether each number is *prime* or *composite*. (Lesson 4-10)

11. 98

12. 61

Tell whether each number is a multiple of 7. Write *yes* or *no*. (Lesson 4-10)

13. 36

14. 84

Use the rule to find the next three terms in the pattern. (Lesson 4-11)

15. 6, 12, 24, 48, …
    Rule: multiply by 2

16. 55, 95, 135, 175, …
    Rule: add 40

17. 4, 12, 36, 108, …
    Rule: multiply by 3

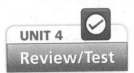
Describe the next term of each pattern. (Lesson 4-11)

18. ▲ ▮ ☐ ▲ ▮ ☐ ▲ ▮ ☐ ▲

_____

19. ◯　　◯　　◯◯　　◯◯
　　◯　◯◯　◯◯　◯◯◯

_____

▶ Problem Solving

For Problems 20–21, write an equation to solve the problem.
(Lessons 4-2, 4-3)

20. The Appalachian Trail is a hiking trail that runs from Maine to Georgia and is approximately 2,160 miles long. Suppose the Andersons want to hike 9 miles per day along an 864-mile section of the trail from New York to Georgia. On how many days will the Andersons hike 9 miles?

_____

_____

21. The library had a large collection of books. Then the librarian ordered 2,200 more books. Now there are 13,327 books. How many books did the library have at the start?

_____

_____

For Problems 22–23, use the pictograph.
Write an equation to solve each
comparison problem. (Lessons 4-4, 4-5, 4-6)

Students' Field Trip Choices	
Zoo	☺ ☺ ☺
Science Center	☺ ☺ ☺ ☺ ☺ ☺
Aquarium	☺ ☺ ☺ ☺ ☺ ☺ ☺
Art Museum	☺ ☺

☺ = 4 votes

22. How many fewer students voted for
the zoo than voted for the aquarium?

_____

23. How many times as many students voted for the
science center as voted for the art museum?

_____

For Problems 24–25, use an equation to solve.
(Lessons 4-7, 4-8, 4-9)

24. Rita and Cody sold refreshments at the football
game. They sold 6 sandwiches, 8 bags of popcorn,
and 20 bottles of water. The sandwiches cost
$5 each. The bags of popcorn cost $2 each.
The bottles of water cost $1 each. How much
money in all did Rita and Cody make?

_____

25. **Extended Response** A bakery had 2 trays with
28 muffins on each tray. The bakery had 4 trays
of cupcakes with 12 cupcakes on each tray.
On Monday, the bakery sold 12 cupcakes.

a. How many muffins and cupcakes were left in all?
Explain.

_____

_____

_____

b. How can you determine if your answer is reasonable?

_____

_____

Dear Family,

This mini-unit is about the metric measurement system. During this unit, students will become familiar with metric units of length, capacity, mass, and time, as well as the size of each when compared to each other.

One **meter** is about the distance an adult man can reach, or a little longer than a yard.

One **liter** is about two large glasses of liquid, or a little more than a quart.

One **gram** is about the mass of a paper clip or a single peanut. One **kilogram** is a little more than 2 pounds.

Students will also discover that the metric system is based on multiples of 10. Prefixes in the names of metric measurements tell the size of a measure compared to the size of the base unit.

Units of Length

kilometer	hectometer	decameter	meter	decimeter	centimeter	millimeter
km	hm	dam	m	dm	cm	mm
10 × 10 × 10 × larger	10 × 10 × larger	10 × larger	1 m	10 × smaller	10 × 10 × smaller	10 × 10 × 10 × smaller
1 km = 1,000 m	1 hm = 100 m	1 dam = 10 m		10 dm = 1 m	100 cm = 1 m	1,000 mm = 1 m

The most commonly used length units are the **kilometer, meter, centimeter,** and **millimeter**.

The most commonly used capacity units are the **liter** and **milliliter**.

The most commonly used units of mass are the **gram, kilogram,** and **milligram**.

If you have any questions or comments, please call or write to me.

Sincerely,
Your child's teacher

COMMON CORE   This unit includes the Common Core Standards for Mathematical Content for Measurement and Data, 4.MD.1, 4.MD.2, 4.MD.3, 4.MD.4 and all Mathematical Practices.

Estimada familia:

Esta mini unidad trata del sistema métrico de medidas. Durante esta unidad, los estudiantes se familiarizarán con unidades métricas de longitud, capacidad y masa, así como con el tamaño de cada una comparada con las otras.

Un **metro** es aproximadamente la distancia que un hombre adulto puede alcanzar extendiendo el brazo, o un poco más de una yarda.

Un **litro** es aproximadamente dos vasos grandes de líquido, o un poco más de un cuarto de galón.

Un **gramo** es aproximadamente la masa de un clip o un cacahuate. Un **kilogramo** es un poco más de 2 libras.

Los estudiantes también descubrirán que el sistema métrico está basado en múltiplos de 10. Los prefijos de los nombres de las medidas métricas indican el tamaño de la medida comparado con el tamaño de la unidad base.

Unidades de longitud						
kilómetro	hectómetro	decámetro	metro	decímetro	centímetro	milímetro
km	hm	dam	m	dm	cm	mm
10 × 10 × 10 × más grande	10 × 10 × más grande	10 × más grande	1 m	10 × más pequeño	10 × 10 × más pequeño	10 × 10 × 10 × más pequeño
1 km = 1,000 m	1 hm = 100 m	1 dam = 10 m		10 dm = 1 m	100 cm = 1 m	1,000 mm = 1 m

Las unidades de longitud más comunes son **kilómetro, metro, centímetro** y **milímetro**.

Las unidades de capacidad más comunes son **litro** y **mililitro**.

Las unidades de masa más comunes son **gramo, kilogramo** y **miligramo**.

Si tiene alguna pregunta o algún comentario, por favor comuníquese conmigo.

Atentamente,
El maestro de su niño

© Houghton Mifflin Harcourt Publishing Company

Esta unidad incluye los Common Core Standards for Mathematical Content for Measurement and Data, 4.MD.1, 4.MD.2, 4.MD.3, 4.MD.4 and all Mathematical Practices.

Measure Length

▶ Convert Metric Units of Measure

You can use a table to convert measurements.

20. How many decimeters are in one meter? _____

21. Complete the equation.
    1 meter = _____ decimeters

22. Complete the table. Explain how you found the number of decimeters in 8 meters.

Meters	Decimeters		
2	2 × 10		= 20
4	___ × 10		= ____
6	6 × ____		= ____
8	_____		= ___

_____

_____

You can also use a number line to convert measurements.

23. Complete the equation. 1 kilometer = _____ meters

24. Label the double number line to show how kilometers (km) and meters (m) are related.

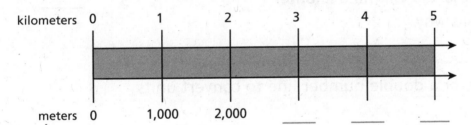

Solve each problem. Label your answers with the correct units.

25. Marsha drove her car 6,835 kilometers last year. How many meters did Marsha drive last year?

    _____

26. John's television is 160 cm wide. How many millimeters wide is the television?

    _____

Solve.

27. 5 m = _____ cm   28. 3 hm = _____ m   29. 7 km = _____ m

Name _____

Date _____

VOCABULARY
liquid volume
liter
milliliter
kiloliter

► Measure Liquid Volume

The base metric unit of **liquid volume** is a **liter**.

Units of Liquid Volume

kiloliter	hectoliter	decaliter	liter	deciliter	centiliter	milliliter
kL	hL	daL	L	dL	cL	mL
10 × 10 × 10 × larger	10 × 10 × larger	10 × larger	1 L	10 × smaller	10 × 10 × smaller	10 × 10 × 10 × smaller
1 kL = 1,000 L	1 hL = 100 L	1 daL = 10 L		10 dL = 1 L	100 cL = 1 L	1,000 mL = 1 L

Ms. Lee's class cut a two-liter plastic bottle in half to make a one-liter jar. They marked the outside to show equal parts.

1. How many **milliliters** of water will fit in the jar?

_____

2. How many of these jars will fill a **kiloliter** container? Explain why.

_____

You can use a table or a double number line to convert units of liquid measure.

3. Complete the table.

Liters	Deciliters	
3	3 × 10	= 30
5	___ × 10	= ___
7	7 × ___	= ___
12	___	= ___

4. Label the double number line to show how liters (L) and milliliters (mL) are related.

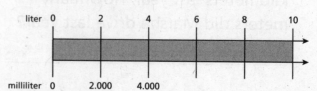

© Houghton Mifflin Harcourt Publishing Company

▶ Vocabulary

Choose the best term from the box.

1. The _____ is the measurement of the distance around the outside of a figure. (Lesson 5-6)

2. One _____ is equal to 16 ounces. (Lesson 5-5)

3. The _____ is the total number of square units inside a figure. (Lesson 5-6)

▶ Concepts and Skills

4. Explain how to find how many cups are in 8 quarts. (Lesson 5-5)

_____

_____

_____

5. Explain why the formula for the per... ~ of a rectangle and the formula for the perimete, ⌐ ~ square are different. (Lesson 5-6)

_____

_____

_____

_____

Convert. (Lessons 5-1, 5-2, 5-3, 5-4, 5-5)

6. 40 m = _____ cm

7. 65 L = _____ cL

8. 3 kg = _____ g

9. 6 yd = _____ ft

10. 3 lb = _____ oz

11. 9 gal = _____ pt

12. 7 hours = _____ min

13. 8 years = ___ months

14. 21 min = _____ sec

Find the area and perimeter of each rectangle. (Lessons 5-6)

15.

6 cm

11 cm

P = _____

A = _____

16.

12 in.

19 in.

P = _____

A = _____

▶ Problem Solving

Solve.   *Show your work.*

17. A movie starts at 12:45 P.M. and is exactly 1 hour and 35 minutes long. What time does the movie end? (Lessons 5-3, 5-7)

_____

18. A rectangular kitchen has an area of 126 square feet. The length is 14 feet. What is the width? (Lesson 5-6, 5-7)

_____

19. Angie buys 6 feet of red ribbon and 8 feet of blue ribbon for a project. How many inches of ribbon did Angie buy in all? (Lessons 5-2, 5-7)

_____

20. **Extended Response** Jack buys some rocks. Each rock has a mass of 4 kilograms. He buys 19 rocks. How many grams of rock did Jack buy? Explain how you solve this problem. (Lessons 5-2, 5-7)

_____

_____

Dear Family,

Your child has experience with fractions through measurements and in previous grades. Unit 6 of *Math Expressions* builds on this experience. The main goals of this unit are to:

- understand the meaning of fractions.
- compare unit fractions.
- add and subtract fractions and mixed numbers with like denominators.
- multiply a fraction by a whole number.

Your child will use fraction bars and fraction strips to gain a visual and conceptual understanding of fractions as parts of a whole. Later, your child will use these models to add and subtract fractions and to convert between improper fractions and mixed numbers.

Examples of Fraction Bar Modeling:

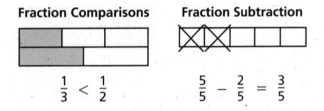

In later lessons of this unit, your child will be introduced to the number line model for fractions. Students name fractions corresponding to given lengths on the number line and identify lengths corresponding to given fractions. They also see that there are many equivalent fraction names for any given length.

Your child will apply this knowledge about fractions and fraction operations to solve real world problems.

If you have questions or problems, please contact me.

Sincerely,
Your child's teacher

This unit includes the Common Core Standards for Mathematical Content for Numbers and Operations-Fractions, 4.NF.3, 4.NF.3a, 4.NF.3b, 4.NF.3c, 4.NF.3d, 4.NF.4a, 4.NF.4b, 4.NF.4c, and all Mathematical Practices.

Estimada familia:

Su niño ha usado fracciones al hacer mediciones y en los grados previos. La Unidad 6 de *Math Expressions* amplía esta experiencia. Los objetivos principales de la unidad son:

- comprender el significado de las fracciones.
- comparar fracciones unitarias.
- sumar y restar fracciones y números mixtos con denominadores iguales.
- multiplicar una fracción por un número entero.

Su niño usará barras y tiras de fracciones para comprender y visualizar el concepto de las fracciones como partes de un entero. Luego, usará estos modelos para sumar y restar fracciones y para convertir fracciones impropias y números mixtos.

Ejemplos de modelos con barras de fracciones:

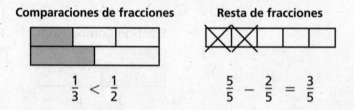

Comparaciones de fracciones   Resta de fracciones

$$\frac{1}{3} < \frac{1}{2} \qquad \frac{5}{5} - \frac{2}{5} = \frac{3}{5}$$

Más adelante en esta unidad, su niño verá el modelo de la recta numérica para las fracciones. Los estudiantes nombrarán las fracciones que correspondan a determinadas longitudes en la recta numérica e identificarán longitudes que corresponden a fracciones dadas. También observarán que hay muchos nombres de fracciones equivalentes para una longitud determinada.

Su niño aplicará este conocimiento de las fracciones y operaciones con fracciones para resolver problemas cotidianos.

Si tiene alguna duda o algún comentario, por favor comuníquese conmigo.

Atentamente,
El máestro de su niño

© Houghton Mifflin Harcourt Publishing Company

COMMON CORE   Esta unidad incluye los Common Core Standards for Mathematical Content for Numbers and Operations-Fractions, 4.NF.3, 4.NF.3a, 4.NF.3b, 4.NF.3c, 4.NF.3d, 4.NF.4a, 4.NF.4b, 4.NF.4c, and all Mathematical Practices.

▶ Sums of Unit Fractions

Shade the fraction bar to show each fraction. Then write the fraction as a sum of unit fractions and as a product of a whole number and a unit fraction. The first one is done for you.

9. $\frac{3}{4}$ = $\frac{1}{4} + \frac{1}{4} + \frac{1}{4}$ = $3 \times \frac{1}{4}$

$\frac{1}{4}$	$\frac{1}{4}$	$\frac{1}{4}$	$\frac{1}{4}$

10. $\frac{3}{8}$ = $\frac{1}{8} + \frac{1}{8} + \frac{1}{8}$ = $3 \times \frac{1}{8}$

$\frac{1}{8}$	$\frac{1}{8}$	$\frac{1}{8}$	$\frac{1}{8}$	$\frac{1}{8}$	$\frac{1}{8}$	$\frac{1}{8}$	$\frac{1}{8}$

11. $\frac{5}{5}$ = $\frac{1}{5} + \frac{1}{5} + \frac{1}{5} + \frac{1}{5} + \frac{1}{5}$ = $5 \times \frac{1}{5}$

$\frac{1}{5}$	$\frac{1}{5}$	$\frac{1}{5}$	$\frac{1}{5}$	$\frac{1}{5}$

12. $\frac{2}{12}$ = $\frac{1}{12} + \frac{1}{12}$ = $2 \times \frac{1}{12}$

$\frac{1}{12}$	$\frac{1}{12}$	$\frac{1}{12}$	$\frac{1}{12}$	$\frac{1}{12}$	$\frac{1}{12}$	$\frac{1}{12}$	$\frac{1}{12}$	$\frac{1}{12}$	$\frac{1}{12}$	$\frac{1}{12}$	$\frac{1}{12}$

13. $\frac{4}{7}$ = $\frac{1}{7} + \frac{1}{7} + \frac{1}{7} + \frac{1}{7}$ = $4 \times \frac{1}{7}$

$\frac{1}{7}$	$\frac{1}{7}$	$\frac{1}{7}$	$\frac{1}{7}$	$\frac{1}{7}$	$\frac{1}{7}$	$\frac{1}{7}$

14. $\frac{7}{9}$ = $\frac{1}{9} + \frac{1}{9} + \frac{1}{9} + \frac{1}{9} + \frac{1}{9} + \frac{1}{9} + \frac{1}{9}$ = $7 \times \frac{1}{9}$

$\frac{1}{9}$	$\frac{1}{9}$	$\frac{1}{9}$	$\frac{1}{9}$	$\frac{1}{9}$	$\frac{1}{9}$	$\frac{1}{9}$	$\frac{1}{9}$	$\frac{1}{9}$

► Fifths that Add to One

Every afternoon, student volunteers help the school librarian put returned books back on the shelves. The librarian puts the books in equal piles on a cart.

One day, Jean and Maria found 5 equal piles on the return cart. They knew there were different ways they could share the job of reshelving the books. They drew fraction bars to help them find all the possibilities.

1. On each fifths bar, circle two groups of fifths to show one way Jean and Maria could share the work. (Each bar should show a different possibility.) Then complete the equation next to each bar to show their shares.

	1 whole	Jean's share	Maria's share

1 whole = all of the books

$\frac{5}{5} = \frac{1}{5} + \frac{4}{5}$

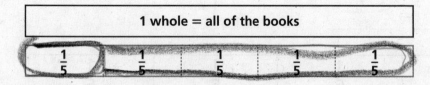

$\frac{5}{5} = \frac{4}{5} + \frac{1}{5}$

$\frac{5}{5} = \frac{2}{5} + \frac{3}{5}$

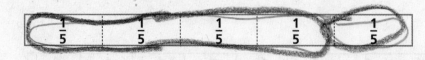

$\frac{5}{5} = \frac{3}{5} + \frac{2}{5}$

▶ Sixths that Add to One

The librarian put 6 equal piles of returned books on the cart for Liu and Henry to reshelf. They also drew fraction bars.

2. On each sixths bar, circle two groups of sixths to show one way that Liu and Henry could share the work. (Each bar should show a different possibility.) Then complete the equation next to each bar to show their shares.

1 whole = all of the books

$\frac{1}{6}$ $\frac{1}{6}$ $\frac{1}{6}$ $\frac{1}{6}$ $\frac{1}{6}$ $\frac{1}{6}$

1 whole   Liu's share   Henry's share

$\frac{6}{6} = \frac{3}{6} + \frac{3}{6}$

$\frac{1}{6}$ $\frac{1}{6}$ $\frac{1}{6}$ $\frac{1}{6}$ $\frac{1}{6}$ $\frac{1}{6}$

$\frac{6}{6} = \frac{4}{6} + \frac{2}{6}$

$\frac{1}{6}$ $\frac{1}{6}$ $\frac{1}{6}$ $\frac{1}{6}$ $\frac{1}{6}$ $\frac{1}{6}$

$\frac{6}{6} = \frac{1}{6} + \frac{5}{6}$

$\frac{1}{6}$ $\frac{1}{6}$ $\frac{1}{6}$ $\frac{1}{6}$ $\frac{1}{6}$ $\frac{1}{6}$

$\frac{6}{6} = \frac{5}{6} + \frac{1}{6}$

$\frac{1}{6}$ $\frac{1}{6}$ $\frac{1}{6}$ $\frac{1}{6}$ $\frac{1}{6}$ $\frac{1}{6}$

$\frac{6}{6} = \frac{2}{6} + \frac{4}{6}$

▶ Find the Unknown Addend

Write the fraction that will complete each equation.

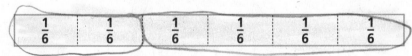

3. $1 = \frac{7}{7} = \frac{1}{7} + \frac{6}{7}$ 4. $1 = \frac{4}{4} = \frac{3}{4} + \frac{1}{4}$

5. $1 = \frac{8}{8} = \frac{3}{8} + \frac{5}{8}$ 6. $1 = \frac{5}{5} = \frac{2}{5} + \frac{3}{5}$

7. $1 = \frac{3}{3} = \frac{2}{3} + \frac{1}{3}$ 8. $1 = \frac{10}{10} = \frac{6}{10} + \frac{4}{10}$

9. $1 = \frac{6}{6} = \frac{2}{6} + \frac{4}{6}$ 10. $1 = \frac{8}{8} = \frac{5}{8} + \frac{3}{8}$

▶ Add Fractions

The circled parts of this fraction bar show an addition problem.

| $\frac{1}{7}$ | $\frac{1}{7}$ | $\frac{1}{7}$ | $\frac{1}{7}$ | $\frac{1}{7}$ | $\frac{1}{7}$ | $\frac{1}{7}$ |

1. Write the numerators that will complete the addition equation.

$$\frac{}{7} + \frac{}{7} = \frac{+}{7} = \frac{}{7}$$

Solve each problem. Write the correct numerator to complete each equation.

2. $\frac{3}{9} + \frac{4}{9} = \frac{+}{9} = \frac{}{9}$ 3. $\frac{1}{5} + \frac{3}{5} = \frac{+}{5} = \frac{}{5}$ 4. $\frac{2}{8} + \frac{5}{8} = \frac{+}{8} = \frac{}{8}$

5. What happens to the numerators in each problem?

_____

6. What happens to the denominators in each problem?

_____

▶ Subtract Fractions

The circled and crossed-out parts of this fraction bar show a subtraction problem.

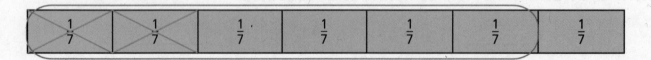

7. Write the numerators that will complete the subtraction equation.

$$\frac{}{7} - \frac{}{7} = \frac{-}{7} = \frac{}{7}$$

Add and Subtract Fractions with Like Denominators

Name _____ Date _____

▶ Practice Addition and Subtraction with Fractions Greater Than 1

Add or subtract.

1. $\frac{8}{5} + \frac{3}{5} =$ _____

2. $\frac{6}{9} + \frac{12}{9} =$ _____

3. $\frac{10}{7} - \frac{3}{7} =$ _____

4. $\frac{10}{8} + \frac{7}{8} =$ _____

5. $\frac{9}{6} - \frac{4}{6} =$ _____

6. $\frac{19}{10} - \frac{7}{10} =$ _____

▶ Add Mixed Numbers with Like Denominators

Add.

7. $2\frac{3}{5}$
   $+ 1\frac{1}{5}$
   _____

8. $1\frac{2}{5}$
   $+ 3\frac{4}{5}$
   _____

9. $3\frac{5}{8}$
   $+ 1\frac{3}{8}$
   _____

10. $5\frac{2}{3}$
    $+ 2\frac{2}{3}$
    _____

▶ Subtract Mixed Numbers with Like Denominators

Subtract.

11. $5\frac{6}{8}$
    $- 3\frac{3}{8}$
    _____

12. $6\frac{2}{8}$
    $- 4\frac{5}{8}$
    _____

13. $4\frac{1}{5}$
    $- 1\frac{3}{5}$
    _____

14. $\frac{1}{}$
    $- 3$
    _____

Explain each solution.

15. $6\frac{2}{7} \overset{5\ \overset{7+2=9}{}}{=} 5\frac{9}{7}$
    $- 1\frac{5}{7} = 1\frac{5}{7}$
    _____
    $\qquad\quad 4\frac{4}{7}$

16. $6\frac{2}{6} \overset{5\ \overset{6+2=8}{}}{=} 5\frac{8}{6}$
    $- 1\frac{5}{6} = 1\frac{5}{6}$
    _____
    $\qquad\quad 4\frac{3}{6}$

17. $6\frac{2}{11} \overset{5\ \overset{11+2=13}{}}{=} 5\frac{13}{11}$
    $- 1\frac{5}{11} = 1\frac{5}{11}$
    _____
    $\qquad\quad 4\frac{8}{11}$

_____

_____

_____

▶ Make a Line Plot

36. Make a mark anywhere on this line segment.

●━━━━━━━━━━━━━━━━━━━●

37. Measure the distance from the left end of the segment to your mark to the nearest quarter inch.

_____

38. Collect measurements from your classmates and record them in the line plot below.

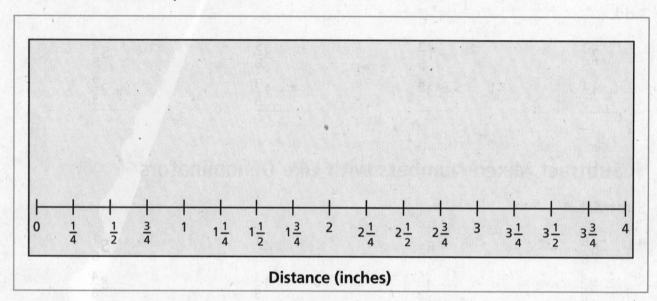

Distance (inches)

39. The range is the difference between the greatest value and the least value. What is the range of the data?

_____

40. Which distance value was most common?

_____

41. Describe any interesting patterns in the data values. For example, are there any large gaps? Are there clusters of values?

_____

_____

© Houghton Mifflin Harcourt Publishing Company
Practice with Fractions and Mixed Numbers

▶ Vocabulary

Choose the best term from the box.

1. A fraction that represents one equal part of a whole is a(n) _____. (Lessons 6-1)

2. A number that consists of a whole number and a fraction is a(n) _____. (Lesson 6-4)

▶ Concepts and Skills

3. Explain how to change $\frac{11}{4}$ to a mixed number. (Lesson 6-4)

_____

_____

4. Elias says the problem below is an addition problem. Vladmir says it is a multiplication problem. Explain why both boys are correct. (Lessons 6-3, 6-7)

Milo practices piano $\frac{2}{3}$ hour every day. How many hours does he practice in 3 days?

_____

_____

Complete. (Lessons 6-1, 6-2, 6-3)

5. $\frac{3}{5} = \frac{1}{5} + \frac{1}{5} +$ _____

6. $\frac{7}{7} = \frac{2}{7} +$ _____

7. $\frac{6}{8} = \frac{4}{8} +$ _____

Write each fraction as a product of a whole number and a unit fraction. (Lessons 6-7, 6-8, 6-9)

8. $\frac{3}{8} =$ _____

9. $\frac{5}{9} =$ _____

Multiply. (Lesson 6-7, 6-8, 6-9)

10. $6 \cdot \frac{1}{5} =$ _____

11. $9 \cdot \frac{1}{3} =$ _____

12. $12 \cdot \frac{3}{4} =$ _____

13. $5 \cdot \frac{4}{7} =$ _____

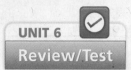

Solve. (Lessons 6-3, 6-4, 6-5, 6-6)

14. $\frac{2}{5} + \frac{1}{5} =$ _____

15. $\frac{7}{9} - \frac{2}{9} =$ _____

16. $\frac{12}{7} + \frac{5}{7} =$ _____

17. $\frac{5}{6} - \frac{4}{6} =$ _____

18. $6\frac{4}{10} - 5\frac{3}{10} =$ _____

19. $4\frac{3}{4} + 3\frac{1}{4} =$ _____

20. $\quad 6\frac{4}{7}$
$\underline{+\ 2\frac{6}{7}}$

21. $\quad 5\frac{4}{9}$
$\underline{-\ 1\frac{7}{9}}$

22. $\quad 3$
$\underline{-\ 1\frac{2}{5}}$

► Problem Solving

Draw a model. Then solve.

23. There is $\frac{3}{4}$ gallon of punch in a bowl. Katie added some punch. Now there is $2\frac{1}{4}$ gallons in the bowl. How much did Katie add? (Lessons 6-5, 6-6, 6-9)

_____

24. Raul ran $\frac{4}{5}$ mile on Tuesday. He ran 4 times this far on Saturday. How far did Raul run on Saturday? (Lessons 6-7, 6-8, 6-9)

_____

25. The line plot shows the lengths of the beads Rachel bought at the bead store today. What is the difference in length between the shortest bead and the longest bead? (Lessons 6-6)

_____

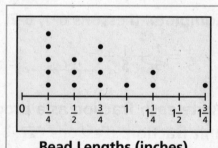

Bead Lengths (inches)

Dear Family,

In Lessons 1 through 7 of Unit 7 of *Math Expressions*, your child will build on previous experience with fractions. Your child will use both physical models and numerical methods to recognize and to find fractions equivalent to a given fraction. Your child will also compare fractions and mixed numbers, including those with like and unlike numerators and denominators.

By using fraction strips students determine how to model and compare fractions, and to find equivalent fractions. Your child will also learn how to use multiplication and division to find equivalent fractions.

Examples of Fraction Bar Modeling:

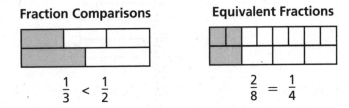

Fraction Comparisons	Equivalent Fractions
$\frac{1}{3} < \frac{1}{2}$	$\frac{2}{8} = \frac{1}{4}$

Your child will be introduced to the number-line model for fractions. Students name fractions corresponding to given lengths on the number line and identify lengths corresponding to given fractions. They also see that there are many equivalent fraction names for any given length.

Your child will apply this knowledge of fractions to word problems and in data displays.

If you have questions or problems, please contact me.

Thank you.

Sincerely,
Your child's teacher

COMMON CORE Lessons 1–7 of this unit include the Common Core Standards for Mathematical Content for Number and Operations—Fractions, 4.NF.1, 4.NF.2, 4.NF.5, 4.MD.4, and all Mathematical Practices.

Estimada familia:

En las lecciones 1 a 7 de la Unidad 7 de *Math Expressions*, el niño ampliará sus conocimientos previos acerca de las fracciones. Su niño usará modelos físicos y métodos numéricos para reconocer y hallar fracciones equivalentes para una fracción dada. También comparará fracciones y números mixtos, incluyendo aquellos que tengan numeradores y denominadores iguales o diferentes.

Usando tiras de fracciones, los estudiantes determinarán cómo hacer modelos y comparar fracciones y cómo hallar fracciones equivalentes. Además, aprenderán cómo usar la multiplicación y división para hallar fracciones equivalentes.

Ejemplos de modelos con barras de fracciones:

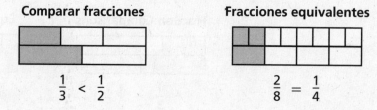

Comparar fracciones $\frac{1}{3} < \frac{1}{2}$ Fracciones equivalentes $\frac{2}{8} = \frac{1}{4}$

Su niño estudiará por primera vez el modelo de recta numérica para las fracciones. Los estudiantes nombrarán las fracciones que correspondan a determinadas longitudes en la recta numérica e identificarán longitudes que correspondan a fracciones dadas. También observarán que hay muchos nombres de fracciones equivalentes para una longitud determinada.

Su niño aplicará este conocimiento de las fracciones en problemas y en presentaciones de datos.

Si tiene alguna duda o algún comentario, por favor comuníquese conmigo.

Atentamente,
El maestro de su niño

COMMON CORE Las lecciones 1 a 7 de esta unidad incluyen los Common Core Standards for Mathematical Content for Number and Operations—Fractions, 4.NF.1, 4.NF.2, 4.NF.5, 4.MD.4 and all Mathematical Practices.

Compare Fractions

| $\frac{1}{1}$ | | | | | | | | | | | | | | | | | | | | $\frac{1}{1}$ |

| $\frac{1}{2}$ | | | | | | | | | | $\frac{1}{2}$ | | | | | | | | | | $\frac{2}{2}$ |

| $\frac{1}{3}$ | | | | | | $\frac{1}{3}$ | | | | | | $\frac{1}{3}$ | | | | | | | | $\frac{3}{3}$ |

| $\frac{1}{4}$ | | | | | $\frac{1}{4}$ | | | | | $\frac{1}{4}$ | | | | | $\frac{1}{4}$ | | | | | $\frac{4}{4}$ |

| $\frac{1}{5}$ | | | | $\frac{1}{5}$ | | | | $\frac{1}{5}$ | | | | $\frac{1}{5}$ | | | | $\frac{1}{5}$ | | | | $\frac{5}{5}$ |

| $\frac{1}{6}$ | | | $\frac{1}{6}$ | | | $\frac{1}{6}$ | | | $\frac{1}{6}$ | | | $\frac{1}{6}$ | | | $\frac{1}{6}$ | | | | | $\frac{6}{6}$ |

| $\frac{1}{7}$ | | $\frac{1}{7}$ | | $\frac{1}{7}$ | | $\frac{1}{7}$ | | $\frac{1}{7}$ | | $\frac{1}{7}$ | | $\frac{1}{7}$ | | | | | | | | $\frac{7}{7}$ |

Bars continue for eighths through twentieths, each bar divided into equal parts labeled $\frac{1}{8}$, $\frac{1}{9}$, $\frac{1}{10}$, $\frac{1}{11}$, $\frac{1}{12}$, $\frac{1}{13}$, $\frac{1}{14}$, $\frac{1}{15}$, $\frac{1}{16}$, $\frac{1}{17}$, $\frac{1}{18}$, $\frac{1}{19}$, $\frac{1}{20}$, with right labels $\frac{8}{8}$, $\frac{9}{9}$, $\frac{10}{10}$, $\frac{11}{11}$, $\frac{12}{12}$, $\frac{13}{13}$, $\frac{14}{14}$, $\frac{15}{15}$, $\frac{16}{16}$, $\frac{17}{17}$, $\frac{18}{18}$, $\frac{19}{19}$, $\frac{20}{20}$.

► Number Lines for Thirds and Sixths

Tell how many equal parts are between zero and 1.
Then write fraction labels above the equal parts.

6. _____

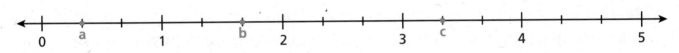

7. _____

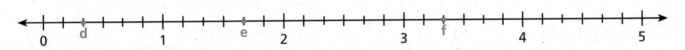

8. _____

Write > or < to make each statement true.

9. $\frac{4}{3}$ ◯ $\frac{7}{6}$ 10. $\frac{8}{3}$ ◯ $\frac{18}{6}$ 11. $3\frac{5}{6}$ ◯ $3\frac{2}{3}$

► Identify Points

12. Write the fraction or mixed number for each lettered
    point above. Describe any patterns you see with the class.

a. _____   b. _____   c. _____

d. _____   e. _____   f. _____

g. _____   h. _____   i. _____

Mark and label the letter of each fraction or
mixed number on the number line.

13.

a. $\frac{1}{5}$ b. $\frac{7}{10}$ c. $1\frac{2}{5}$ d. $2\frac{1}{2}$

e. $3\frac{3}{10}$ f. $4\frac{2}{5}$ g. $4\frac{9}{10}$ h. $5\frac{1}{2}$

VOCABULARY
simplify

▶ Simplify Fractions

Simplifying a fraction means finding an equivalent fraction with a lesser numerator and denominator. Simplifying a fraction results in an equivalent fraction with fewer but greater unit fractions.

1. Maria had 12 boxes of apricots. She sold 10 of the boxes. Write the fraction of the boxes sold, and lightly shade the twelfths fraction bar to show this fraction.

   Fraction sold: $\frac{10}{12}$ _____

2. Group the twelfths to form an equivalent fraction with a lesser denominator. Show the new fraction by dividing, labeling, and lightly shading the blank fraction bar.

   Fraction sold: _____

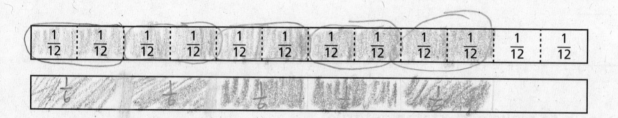

3. In Problem 2, you formed groups of twelfths to get a greater unit fraction. How many twelfths are in each group? In other words, what is the *group size*?

   _____ 2 _____

4. Show how you can find the equivalent fraction by dividing the numerator and denominator by the group size.

   $$\frac{10}{12} = \frac{10 \div \boxed{2}}{12 \div \boxed{2}} = \frac{\boxed{5}}{\boxed{6}}$$

Use what you know to find these equivalent fractions. You may want to sketch a thirds fraction bar below the two fraction bars above.

5. $\frac{8}{12} = \frac{\boxed{4}}{6} = \frac{\boxed{2}}{3}$

6. $\frac{4}{12} = \frac{\boxed{2}}{6} = \frac{\boxed{1}}{3}$

7. $\frac{20}{12} = \frac{\boxed{10}}{6} = \frac{\boxed{5}}{3} = \boxed{1}\frac{\boxed{2}}{3}$

© Houghton Mifflin Harcourt Publishing Company

Equivalent Fractions Using Division

▶ Use Fraction Bars to Find Equivalent Fractions

8. Look at the thirds bar. Circle enough unit fractions on each of the other bars to equal $\frac{1}{3}$.

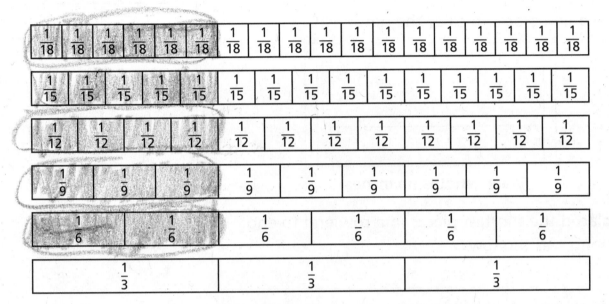

9. Discuss how the parts of the fraction bars you circled show this chain of equivalent fractions. Explain how each different group of unit fractions is equal to $\frac{1}{3}$.

$$\frac{6}{18} \quad = \quad \frac{5}{15} \quad = \quad \frac{4}{12} \quad = \quad \frac{3}{9} \quad = \quad \frac{2}{6} \quad = \quad \frac{1}{3}$$

_____

_____

10. Write the group size for each fraction in the chain of equivalent fractions. The first one is done for you.

   6   ___   ___   ___   ___   ___

11. Complete each equation by showing how you use group size to simplify. The first one is done for you.

$$\frac{6 \div 6}{18 \div 6} = \frac{1}{3} \qquad \frac{5 \div 5}{15 \div 5} = \frac{1}{3} \qquad \frac{4 \div 4}{12 \div 4} = \frac{1}{3}$$

$$\frac{3 \div 3}{9 \div 3} = \frac{1}{3} \qquad \frac{2 \div 2}{6 \div 2} = \frac{1}{3}$$

► Make a Line Plot

Mai cut up strips of color paper to make a collage. The lengths of the unused pieces are shown in the table.

Length (in inches)	Number of Pieces
$\frac{1}{2}$	4
$\frac{5}{8}$	2
$\frac{3}{4}$	2
$\frac{7}{8}$	3
$1\frac{1}{4}$	2

7. Make a line plot to display the data.

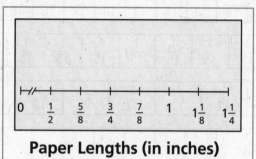

Paper Lengths (in inches)

8. Mai placed the shortest pieces in a row end to end. How long was the row?

_____

A group of students measured the widths of their hands. The measurements are shown in the table.

Width (in inches)	Number of Students
$2\frac{1}{4}$	1
$2\frac{3}{8}$	2
$2\frac{1}{2}$	2
$2\frac{5}{8}$	4
$2\frac{3}{4}$	2
$2\frac{7}{8}$	1

9. Make a line plot to display the data.

```
   0  2 1/4  2 3/8  2 1/2  2 5/8  2 3/4  2 7/8
```

Hand Width (in inches)

10. What is the difference between the width of the widest hand and the most common hand width?

_____

11. Write a problem you could solve by using the line plot.

_____

_____

_____

Fractions and Line Plots

Dear Family,

In this unit, your child will be introduced to decimal numbers. Students will begin by using what they already know about pennies, dimes, and dollars to see connections between fractions and decimals.

Students will explore decimal numbers by using bars divided into tenths and hundredths. They will relate decimals to fractions, which are also used to represent parts of a whole.

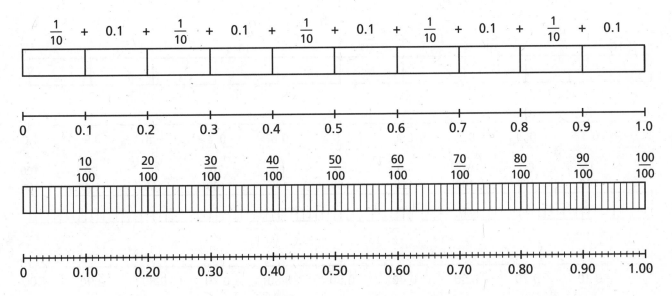

Students will read, write, and model decimal numbers. They will also learn to combine whole numbers with decimals. They will work with numbers such as 1.72 and 12.9. Students will also compare decimal numbers with other decimal numbers.

Students will apply their understanding of decimal concepts when they compare decimals.

Comparing Decimals

6.8 ◯ 3.42   6.80 (>) 3.42

Adding a zero makes the numbers easier to compare.

Please call if you have any questions or comments.

Thank you.

Sincerely,
Your child's teacher

COMMON CORE This unit includes the Common Core Standards for Mathematical Content for Number and Operations–Fractions, and Measurement and Data, 4.NF.1, 4.NF.2, 4.NF.6, 4.NF.7, 4.MD.2, 4.MD.4, and all Mathematical Practices.

Carta a la familia

Estimada familia:

En esta unidad, se presentarán los números decimales. Para comenzar, los estudiantes usarán lo que ya saben acerca de las monedas de un centavo, de las monedas de diez y de los dólares, para ver cómo se relacionan las fracciones y los decimales.

Los estudiantes estudiarán los números decimales usando barras divididas en décimos y centésimos. Relacionarán los decimales con las fracciones que también se usan para representar partes del entero.

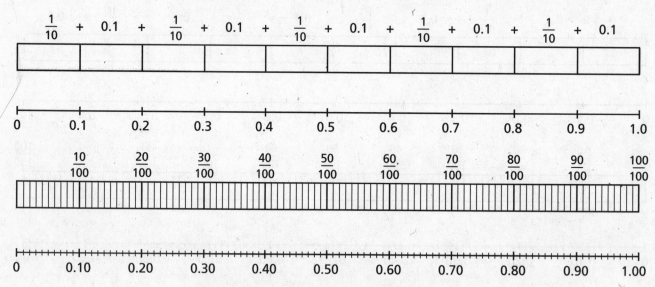

$\frac{1}{10}$ + 0.1 + $\frac{1}{10}$ + 0.1 + $\frac{1}{10}$ + 0.1 + $\frac{1}{10}$ + 0.1 + $\frac{1}{10}$ + 0.1

| 0 | 0.1 | 0.2 | 0.3 | 0.4 | 0.5 | 0.6 | 0.7 | 0.8 | 0.9 | 1.0 |

$\frac{10}{100}$ $\frac{20}{100}$ $\frac{30}{100}$ $\frac{40}{100}$ $\frac{50}{100}$ $\frac{60}{100}$ $\frac{70}{100}$ $\frac{80}{100}$ $\frac{90}{100}$ $\frac{100}{100}$

| 0 | 0.10 | 0.20 | 0.30 | 0.40 | 0.50 | 0.60 | 0.70 | 0.80 | 0.90 | 1.00 |

Los estudiantes leerán, escribirán y representarán números decimales. También aprenderán a combinar números enteros con decimales. Trabajarán con números tales como 1.72 y 12.9. Compararán números decimales con otros números decimales.

Al comparar decimales, los estudiantes aplicarán los conceptos decimales que ya conozcan.

Comparar decimales

6.8 ◯ 3.42   6.80 ⟨>⟩ 3.42

Añadir un cero facilita la comparación de números.

Si tiene alguna duda o algún comentario, por favor comuníquese conmigo.

Gracias.

Atentamente,
El maestro de su niño

COMMON CORE

Esta unidad incluye los Common Core Standards for Mathematical Content for Number and Operations–Fractions, and Measurement and Data, 4.NF.1, 4.NF.2, 4.NF.6, 4.NF.7, 4.MD.2, 4.MD.4, and all Mathematical Practices.

Relate Fractions and Decimals

Name _____ **Date** _____

▶ Model Equivalent Fractions and Decimals

Write a fraction and a decimal to represent the shaded part of each whole.

15.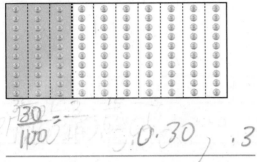

$\frac{30}{100} =$

0.30 , $.3$

16.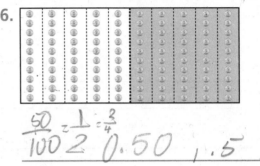

$\frac{50}{100} = \frac{1}{2} = \frac{3}{4}$

0.50 , $.5$

Divide each whole and use shading to show the given fraction or decimal.

17. 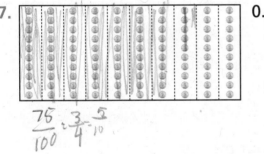   0.75

$\frac{75}{100} = \frac{3}{4} = \frac{5}{10}$

18. 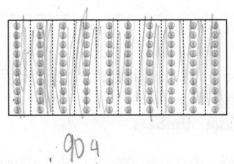 $\frac{9}{10}$

$.904$

1.5 , 1.50

Shade these grids to show that $\frac{3}{2} = 1\frac{1}{2}$.

19.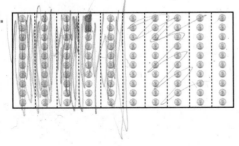

VOCABULARY
tenths
hundredths
decimal number

► Understand Tenths and Hundredths

Answer the questions about the bars and number lines below.

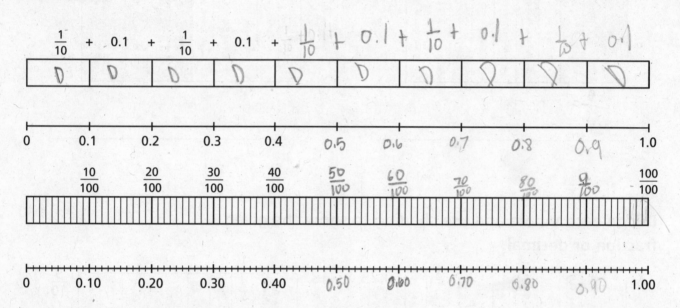

$\frac{1}{10}$ + 0.1 + $\frac{1}{10}$ + 0.1 + $\frac{1}{10}$ + 0.1 + $\frac{1}{10}$ + 0.1 + $\frac{1}{10}$ + 0.1

| D | D | D | D | D | D | D | D | D | D |

0   0.1   0.2   0.3   0.4   0.5   0.6   0.7   0.8   0.9   1.0

$\frac{10}{100}$ $\frac{20}{100}$ $\frac{30}{100}$ $\frac{40}{100}$ $\frac{50}{100}$ $\frac{60}{100}$ $\frac{70}{100}$ $\frac{80}{100}$ $\frac{9}{100}$ $\frac{100}{100}$

0   0.10   0.20   0.30   0.40   0.50   0.60   0.70   0.80   0.90   1.00

1. The bars show **tenths** and **hundredths**. Finish labeling the bars and number lines using fractions and **decimal numbers**.

2. Use what you know about fractions and about money (a dime = one tenth of a dollar and a penny = one hundredth of a dollar) to explain why 3 tenths is the same as 30 hundredths.

   There equivilent fractions ex. → $\frac{3}{10} = \frac{30}{100} = \frac{30 \div 10}{100 \div 10} = \frac{3}{10}$

   $\frac{3}{10} = \frac{3 \times 10}{10 \times 10} = \frac{30}{100} =$

3. Tenths are greater than hundredths even though 10 is less than 100. Explain why this is true.

   Dime is bigger than a Penny.

   ten
   tenth
   hundred   hundreth

© Houghton Mifflin Harcourt Publishing Company

Explore Decimal Numbers

Name _____ **Date** _____

▶ Discuss Symmetry Around the Ones

◄──── × 10 (Greater) ──────────────── ÷ 10 (Lesser) ────►

Hundreds	Tens	ONES	Tenths	Hundredths
100.	10.	1.	0.1	0.01
$\dfrac{100}{1}$	$\dfrac{10}{1}$	$\dfrac{1}{1}$	$\dfrac{1}{10}$	$\dfrac{1}{100}$
$100.00	$10.00	$1.00	$0.10	$0.01

1. Discuss symmetries and relationships you see in the place value chart.

2. Is it easier to see place value patterns in **a** or **b**? Discuss why.

   a. 500   50   5   .5   .05

   b. 500   50   5   0.5   0.05

▶ Show and Read Decimal Numbers

Use your Decimal Secret Code Cards to make numbers on the frame.

Place value	Hundreds	Tens	ONES	Tenths	Hundredths
Make numbers					
Read numbers			•	and tenths	hundredths

Name _____ Date _____

▶ Write Numbers in Decimal Form

Read and write each mixed number as a decimal.

3. $3\frac{1}{10}$ _____

4. $5\frac{7}{100}$ _____

5. $2\frac{46}{100}$ _____

6. $28\frac{9}{10}$ _____

Read and write each decimal as a mixed number.

7. 12.8 _____

8. 3.05 _____

9. 4.85 _____

10. 49.7 _____

**Read each word name. Then write a decimal
for each word name.**

11. sixty-one hundredths

_____

12. six and fourteen hundredths

_____

13. seventy and eight tenths

_____

14. fifty-five and six hundredths

_____

▶ Expanded Form

Write each decimal in expanded form.

15. 8.2 _____

16. 17.45 _____

17. 106.24 _____

18. 50.77 _____

19. 312.09 _____

20. 693.24 _____

Solve.

21. There are 100 centimeters in
1 meter. A snake crawls 3 meters
and 12 more centimeters. What
decimal represents the number of
meters the snake crawls?

_____

22. There are 100 pennies in 1 dollar.
A jar contains 20 dollars. You add
8 pennies to the jar. What decimal
represents the number of dollars in
the jar?

_____

Name _____   **Date** _____

▶ Decimal Secret Code Cards

100	10	1
1 0 0	1 0	1
200	20	2
2 0 0	2 0	2
300	30	3
3 0 0	3 0	3
400	40	4
4 0 0	4 0	4
500	50	5
5 0 0	5 0	5
600	60	6
6 0 0	6 0	6
700	70	7
7 0 0	7 0	7
800	80	8
8 0 0	8 0	8
900	90	9
9 0 0	9 0	9

▶ Decimal Secret Code Cards

| $1 | $10 | $100 |

| $1 | $10 | $100 |
| $1 | $10 | $100 |

$1	$10	$100
$1	$10	$100
$1	$10	$100

$1	$10	$100
$1	$10	$100
$1	$10	$100
$1	$10	$100

$1	$10	$100
$1	$10	$100
$1	$10	$100
$1	$10	$100
$1	$10	$100

$1	$1	$10	$10	$100	$100
$1		$10		$100	
$1		$10		$100	
$1		$10		$100	
$1		$10		$100	

$1	$1	$10	$10	$100	$100
$1	$1	$10	$10	$100	$100
$1		$10		$100	
$1		$10		$100	
$1		$10		$100	

$1	$1	$10	$10	$100	$100
$1	$1	$10	$10	$100	$100
$1	$1	$10	$10	$100	$100
$1		$10		$100	
$1		$10		$100	

$1	$1	$10	$10	$100	$100
$1	$1	$10	$10	$100	$100
$1	$1	$10	$10	$100	$100
$1	$1	$10	$10	$100	$100
$1		$10		$100	

VOCABULARY
common denominator
decimal number
equivalent fractions
line plot

► Vocabulary

Choose the best term from the box.

1. _____ are two or more fractions that represent the same part of a whole. (Lesson 7-4)

2. A graph that shows data on a number line is a _____. (Lesson 7-7)

3. A _____ is separated by a decimal point and shows the whole-number part on the left and the fraction part on the right. (Lesson 7-9)

► Concepts and Skills

4. Leonard bought a large water bottle and Natasha bought a small water bottle. They each drank $\frac{1}{2}$ of their bottles. Did they drink the same amount? Explain. (Lesson 7-3)

_____

_____

_____

5. Explain how to compare $\frac{3}{4}$ and $\frac{3}{5}$. (Lesson 7-1)

_____

_____

_____

6. Is $\frac{1}{4}$ equivalent to $\frac{3}{8}$? Explain. (Lesson 7-4)

_____

_____

_____

Simplify each fraction. (Lesson 7-5)

7. $\frac{9}{12}$ = _____

8. $\frac{15}{40}$ = _____

9. Write 5 fractions that are equivalent to $\frac{1}{5}$. (Lesson 7-4)

_____ _____ _____ _____ _____

10. Label the point for each fraction or mixed number with the corresponding letter. (Lesson 7-2)

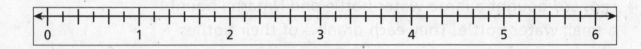

a. $1\frac{2}{3}$ b. $5\frac{1}{6}$ c. $\frac{1}{2}$ d. $3\frac{5}{6}$ e. $4\frac{1}{3}$

Which fraction is closest to 4? _____

Write each number in decimal form. (Lessons 7-9, 7-11)

11. seventy-four hundredths

_____

12. $8\frac{3}{10}$

_____

13. $12\frac{4}{100}$

_____

14. twenty-one and thirty-five hundredths

_____

Write >, <, or = to make each statement true. (Lessons 7-6, 7-10, 7-12)

15. $\frac{3}{4}$ ◯ $\frac{8}{12}$ 16. $\frac{2}{3}$ ◯ $\frac{6}{9}$

17. 0.7 ◯ 0.75   18. 0.4 ◯ 0.25

19. 8.04 ◯ 8.40   20. 50.07 ◯ 5.70

▶ Problem Solving

Solve.

21. A farm stand sells cartons of blueberries by weight.
The stand weighs each carton to determine its price.
The data show the weights of the cartons of blueberries
that the stand is selling. (Lesson 7-7)

a. Make a line plot to display the data.

Weight (in pounds)	Number of Cartons
$\frac{1}{4}$	2
$\frac{1}{2}$	3
$\frac{3}{4}$	5
1	3
$1\frac{1}{4}$	1

b. What general statement can you make about
the weights of the blueberry cartons?

_____

_____

_____

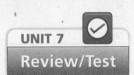
22. The shaded part of the model represents the number of   *Show your work.*
    pennies Nate has in his jar. Write the number of pennies
    Nate has in his jar as a fraction and as a decimal. (Lesson 7-8)

 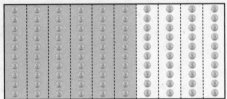

_____

23. A pad of paper has 100 sheets. Helena has 4 full pads
    and 53 loose sheets of paper. What decimal number
    represents the number of sheets of paper Helena has?
    (Lesson 7-11)

_____

24. Vaughn bought 10 tomato seedlings. He has 7 seedlings
    that are cherry tomatoes and the rest are plum tomatoes.
    What decimal number shows the fraction of tomatoes
    that are plum tomatoes? (Lesson 7-9)

_____

25. **Extended Response** Four track team members run in
    the 200-meter relay race. Kaya ran 200-meters in
    31.09 seconds. Both Sara and Min ran 200-meters in
    31.9 seconds. Lana ran the race in 31.90 seconds.
    Did all of the team members run the race in the
    same amount of time? Explain. (Lesson 7-12)

_____

_____

_____

_____

_____

Dear Family,

In the first half of Unit 8, your child will be learning to recognize and describe geometric figures. One type of figure is an angle. Your child will use a protractor to find the measures of angles.

Other figures, such as triangles, may be named based on their angles and sides.

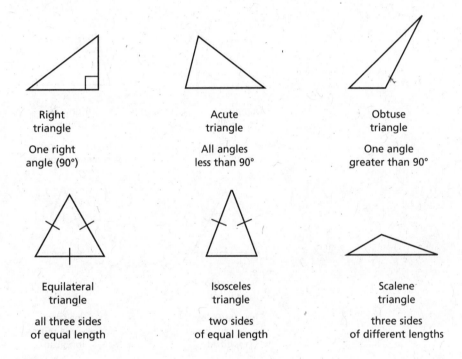

Right triangle	Acute triangle	Obtuse triangle
One right angle (90°)	All angles less than 90°	One angle greater than 90°

Equilateral triangle	Isosceles triangle	Scalene triangle
all three sides of equal length	two sides of equal length	three sides of different lengths

Be sure that your child continues to review and practice the basics of multiplication and division. A good understanding of the basics will be very important in later math courses when students learn more difficult concepts in multiplication and division.

If you have any questions or comments, please call or write to me.

Thank you.

Sincerely,
Your child's teacher

COMMON CORE This unit includes the Common Core Standards for Mathematical Content for Measurement and Data, 4.MD.5, 4.MD.5a, 4.MD.5b, 4.MD.6, 4.MD.7; Geometry, 4.G.1, 4.G.2; and all the Mathematical Practices.

Estimada familia:

En la primera parte de la Unidad 8, su niño aprenderá a reconocer y a describir figuras geométricas. Un ángulo es un tipo de figura. Su niño usará un transportador para hallar las medidas de los ángulos.

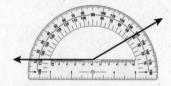

Otras figuras, tales como los triángulos, se nombran según sus ángulos y lados.

Triángulo rectángulo

Tiene un ángulo recto (90°)

Triángulo acutángulo

Todos los ángulos son menores que 90°

Triángulo obtusángulo

Tiene un ángulo mayor que 90°

Triángulo equilátero

los tres lados tienen la misma longitud

Triángulo isósceles

dos lados tienen la misma longitud

Triángulo escaleno

los tres lados tienen diferente longitud

Asegúrese de que su niño siga repasando y practicando las multiplicaciones y divisiones básicas. Es importante que domine las operaciones básicas para que, en los cursos de matemáticas de más adelante, pueda aprender conceptos de multiplicación y división más difíciles.

Si tiene alguna pregunta o algún comentario, por favor comuníquese conmigo.

Gracias.

Atentamente,

El maestro de su niño

COMMON CORE Esta unidad incluye los Common Core Standards for Mathematical Content for Measurement and Data, 4.MD.5, 4.MD.5a, 4.MD.5b, 4.MD.6, 4.MD.7; Geometry, 4.G.1, 4.G.2; and all the Mathematical Practices.

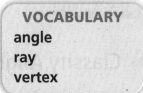

▶ Drawing Points, Rays, and Angles

An **angle** is formed by two **rays** with the same endpoint, called the **vertex**.

You can label figures with letters to name them. This is ∠ABC. Its rays are $\overrightarrow{BA}$ and $\overrightarrow{BC}$.

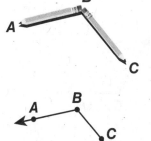

Draw and label each figure.

2. Draw and label a point. Write the name of your point. _____

3. Draw a ray. Label the endpoint. Write the name of your ray. _____

4. Draw an angle. Label the vertex and the two rays. Write the name of your angle. _____

► Classify Angles

Use the letters to name each angle. Then write *acute*, *right*, or *obtuse* to describe each angle.

10.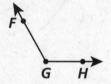

_____

_____

11.

_____

_____

12.

_____

_____

13. Use the letters to name two acute and two obtuse angles in this figure. Write *acute* or *obtuse* to describe each angle.

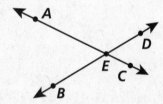

_____

_____

_____

_____

14. Draw and label a right angle, an acute angle, and an obtuse angle.

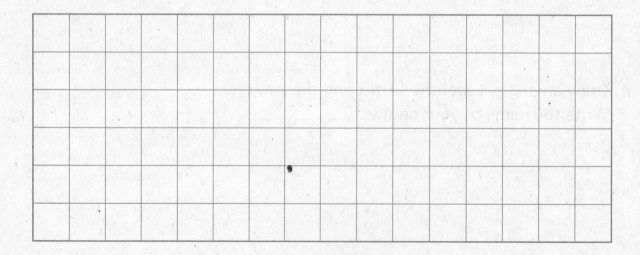

► **Sort Angles**

Cut along the dashed lines.

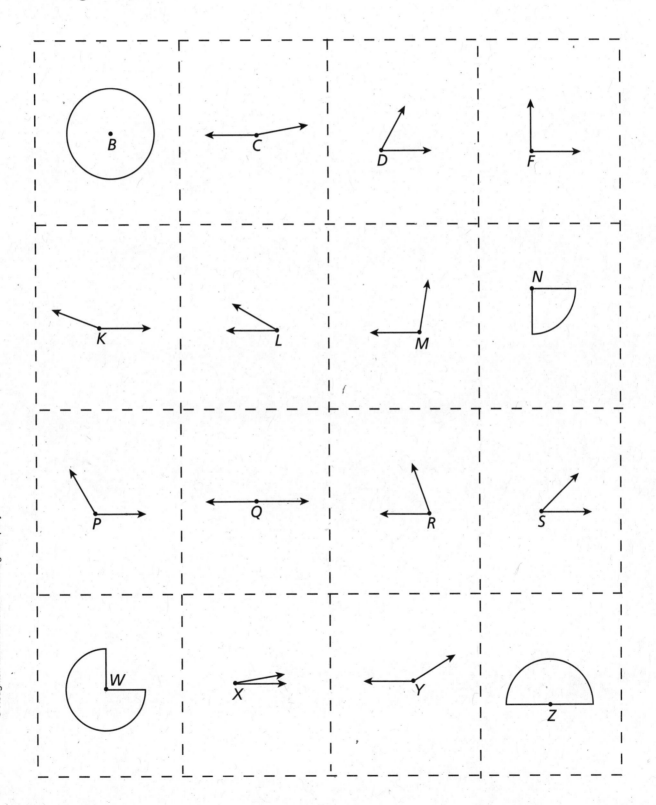

Name _____

Date _____

▶ Use a Protractor

A **protractor** is a tool that is used to measure angles in degrees. This protractor shows that ∠ABC measures 90°.

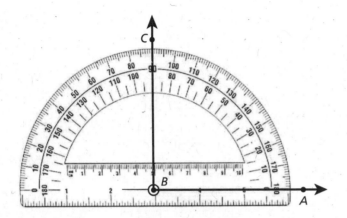

Measure each angle with your protractor. Write the measure.

1.

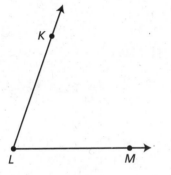

∠KLM = _____

2.

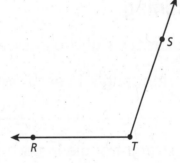

∠STR = _____

3.

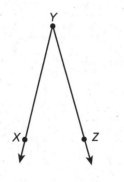

∠XYZ = _____

4.

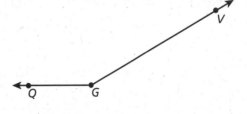

∠QGV = _____

▶ Sketch Angles

Sketch each angle, or draw it using a protractor.

5.   90°

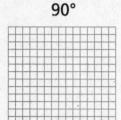

6.   45°

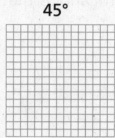

7.   180°

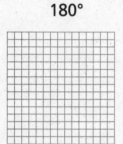

8.   360°

▶ Use Reasoning

Use the figures at the right to answer the following questions.

9. Name one right angle in each figure.

   _____

10. Name one straight angle in each figure.

    _____

11. How much greater is the measure of
    ∠KRB than the measure of ∠IAO?

    _____

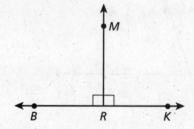

12. Which angle appears to be a 45° angle?

    _____

13. The measure of ∠IAE is 135°.

    What is the measure of ∠OAE? _____

    What is the measure of ∠UAE? _____

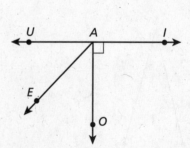

Name

Date

▶ Draw Angles in a Circle

Use a straightedge and a protractor to draw and shade
an angle of each type. Measure and label each angle.

1. obtuse angle

2. straight angle

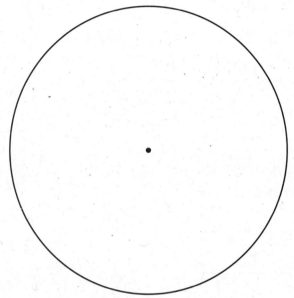
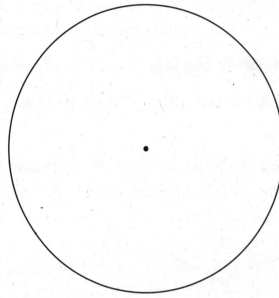

3. acute angle

4. three angles with a sum of 360°

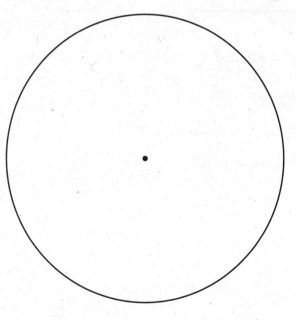
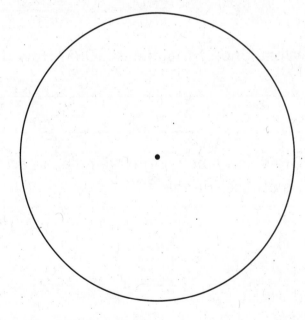

5. Write out the sum of your angle measures in Exercise 4
   to show that it equals 360°

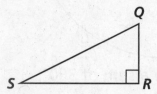

VOCABULARY
right triangle
obtuse triangle
acute triangle

▶ Discuss Angles of a Triangle

The prefix *tri-* means "three," so it is easy to remember that a triangle has 3 angles. Triangles can take their names from the kind of angles they have.

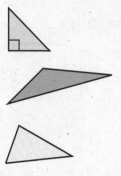

- A **right triangle** has one right angle, which we show by drawing a small square at the right angle.

- An **obtuse triangle** has one obtuse angle.

- An **acute triangle** has three acute angles.

1. You can also use letters to write and talk about triangles. This triangle is △*QRS*. Name its three angles and their type.

_____

_____

_____

2. What kind of triangle is △*QRS*? How do you know?

_____

_____

3. Draw and label a right triangle, an acute triangle, and an obtuse triangle.

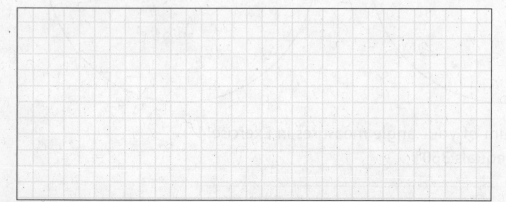

Name Triangles

© Houghton Mifflin Harcourt Publishing Company

Dear Family,

Your child has been learning about geometry throughout this unit. In this second half of the unit, your child will be learning how to recognize and describe a group of geometric figures called quadrilaterals, which get their name because they have four (*quad-*) sides (*-lateral*). Five different kinds of quadrilaterals are shown here.

Square
4 equal sides
opposite sides parallel
4 right angles

Rectangle
2 pairs of parallel sides
4 right angles

Rhombus
4 equal sides
opposite sides parallel

Parallelogram
2 pairs of parallel sides

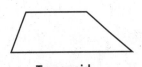

Trapezoid
exactly 1 pair of opposite sides parallel

If you have any questions or comments, please call or write to me.

Sincerely,
Your child's teacher

COMMON CORE This unit includes the Common Core Standards for Mathematical Content for Operations and Algebraic Thinking, 4.OA.5; Geometry, 4.G.1, 4.G.2, 4.G.3; and all the Mathematical Practices.

Carta a la familia

Estimada familia:

Durante esta unidad, su niño ha estado aprendiendo acerca de geometría. En esta parte de la unidad, su niño aprenderá cómo reconocer y describir un grupo de figuras geométricas llamadas cuadriláteros, que reciben ese nombre porque tienen cuatro *(quadri-)* lados *(-lateris)*. Aquí se muestran cinco tipos de cuadriláteros:

Cuadrado
4 lados iguales
lados opuestos paralelos
4 ángulos rectos

Rectángulo
2 pares de lados paralelos
4 ángulos rectos

Rombo
4 lados iguales
lados opuestos paralelos

Paralelogramo
2 pares de lados paralelos

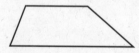

Trapecio
exactamente 1 par de lados paralelos opuestos

Si tiene alguna pregunta o algún comentario, por favor comuníquese conmigo.

Atentamente,
El maestro de su niño

© Houghton Mifflin Harcourt Publishing Company

COMMON CORE Esta unidad incluye los Common Core Standards for Mathematical Content for Operations and Algebraic Thinking, 4.OA.5; Geometry, 4.G.1, 4.G.2, 4.G.3; and all the Mathematical Practices.

106 UNIT 8 LESSON 7

Parallel and Perpendicular Lines and Line Segments

VOCABULARY
parallel

▶ Define Parallel Lines

The lines or line segments in these pairs are **parallel**.

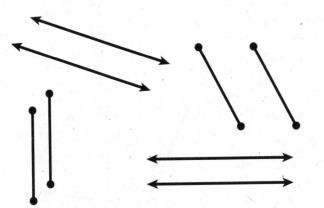

The lines or line segments in these pairs are not parallel.

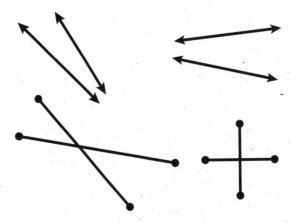

1. What do you think it means for two lines to be parallel?

_____

_____

▶ Draw Parallel Lines

2. Draw and label a pair of parallel lines.

3. Draw and label a figure with one pair of parallel line segments.

VOCABULARY
perpendicular

▶ Define Perpendicular Lines

The lines or line segments in these pairs are **perpendicular**.

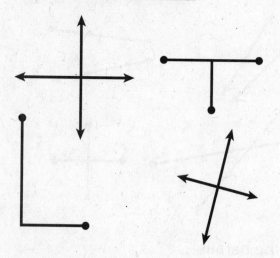

The lines or line segments in these pairs are not perpendicular.

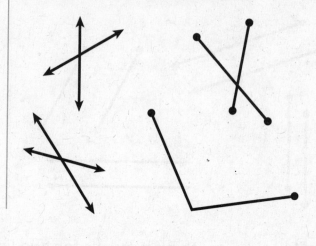

4. What do you think it means for two lines to be perpendicular?

_____

_____

▶ Draw Perpendicular Lines

5. Draw and label a pair of perpendicular lines.

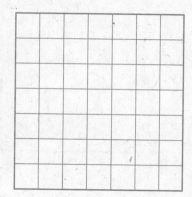

6. Draw and label a figure with one pair of perpendicular line segments.

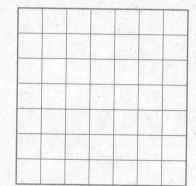

▶ Draw Special Quadrilaterals

5. Draw a quadrilateral that has exactly one pair of opposite sides parallel. What type of quadrilateral is it?

_____trapizode_____

6. Draw a quadrilateral that has two pairs of opposite sides parallel. What type of quadrilateral is it? Is there more than one answer?

_____rectangle, square, rhombus_____

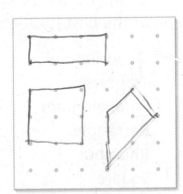

7. Draw a quadrilateral that has two pairs of opposite sides parallel, 4 equal sides, and no right angles. What type of quadrilateral is it?

_____rhombus_____

Name _____   **Date** _____

▶ Identify Relationships

Why is each statement below true?

8. A rhombus is always a parallelogram, but a parallelogram isn't always a rhombus.

9. A rectangle is a parallelogram, but a parallelogram is not necessarily a rectangle. *True because it has to have Right angles.*

10. A square is a rectangle, but a rectangle does not have to be a square.

11. Complete the category diagram by placing each word in the best location.

Quadrilateral
Trapezoid
Parallelogram
Rectangle
Rhombus
Square

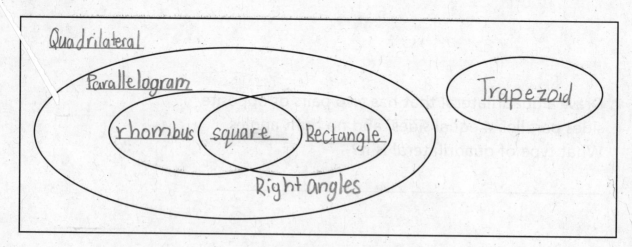

Classify Quadrilaterals

Name _____   Date _____

► Sort and Classify Quadrilaterals

Cut along the dashed lines.

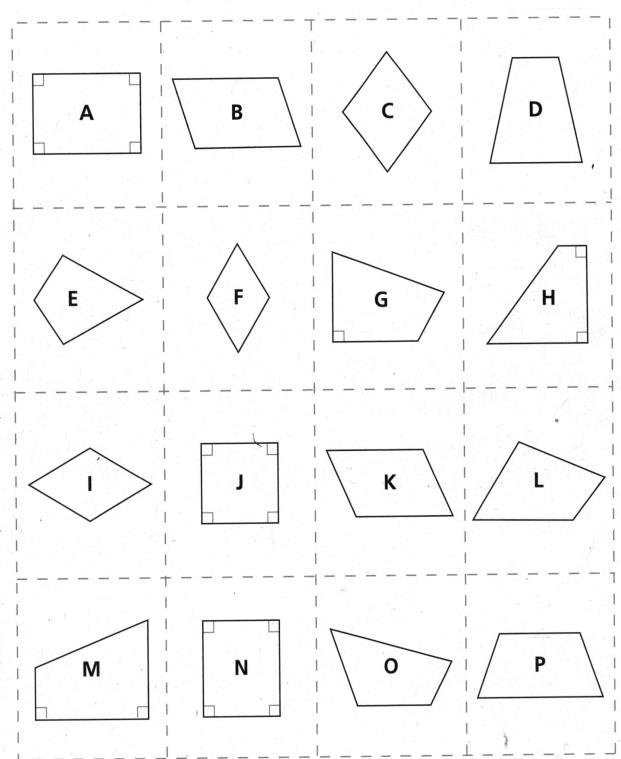

Classify Quadrilaterals

Name _____   Date _____

▶ Sort Polygons Cards

A	B	C
D	E	F
G	H	I
J	K	L
M	N	O

Classify Polygons

VOCABULARY
acute angle
degree
parallel
perpendicular

► Vocabulary

Choose the best term from the box.

1. A _____ is $\frac{1}{360}$th of a circle. (Lesson 8-2)

2. Two lines are _____ if they form a right angle. (Lesson 8-7)

3. An _____ has a measure less than 90°. (Lesson 8-1)

► Concepts and Skills

4. Explain how you would use a protractor to measure the angle at the right. What is the angle measure? (Lesson 8-2)

_____

_____

_____

5. Look at the figures below. Circle the figures that have parallel lines. (Lesson 8-10)

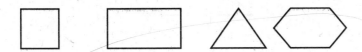

6. Look at the figures below. Circle the figures that have acute angles. (Lesson 8-10)

Draw each figure. (Lesson 8-1)

7. Line *AB*

8. Line segment *FG*

Tell whether each pair of lines is parallel or perpendicular. (Lesson 8-7)

9.

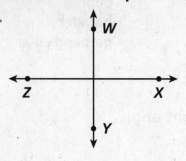

_____

10.

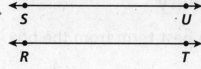

_____

Measure the angle. Tell if it is an acute, obtuse, or right angle. (Lesson 8-2)

11.

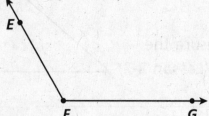

_____

12.

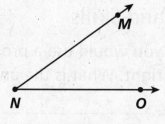

_____

Name each triangle by its sides. (Lesson 8-4)

13.

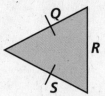

_____

14.

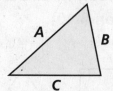

_____

List all names for the quadrilateral. Then use letters to name the triangles you can make with the diagonals and write the type of triangles. (Lessons 8-8, 8-9)

15.

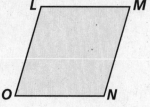

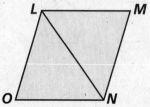

_____

_____

_____

_____

Draw all of the lines of symmetry for each figure. (Lesson 8-11)

16.

17.

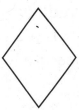

▶ Problem Solving

Use the map to solve each problem. (Lessons 8-4, 8-6, 8-7)

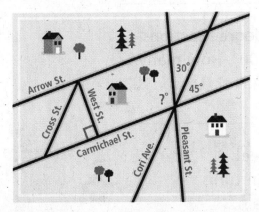

18. Suli and Ty are walking along parallel streets. Which two streets in the map appear to be parallel?

_____

19. Cross Street, West Street, and Carmichael Street form a triangle around a park. Classify the triangle formed by these streets by its sides and its angles.

_____

20. What is the measure of the obtuse angle formed by Pleasant Street and Carmichael Street?

_____

21. Which two streets are perpendicular?

_____

Solve each problem.

Show your work.

22. Lucy is designing a block for a quilt. She measured one of the angles. What is the unknown angle measure? (Lessons 8-5, 8-6)

_____

23. A tile has two pairs of parallel sides and two pairs of equal sides. What shape is the tile? (Lesson 8-8)

_____

24. A gear in a watch turns in one-degree sections. The gear has turned a total of 300°. How many one-degree turns did the gear make? (Lesson 8-3)

_____

25. **Extended Response** A Ferris wheel turns 35° before it pauses. It then turns another 85° before stopping again. What is the total measure of the angle that the Ferris wheel turned? How many more times will it need to repeat the pattern to turn 360°? Explain your thinking. (Lessons 8-2, 8-3, 8-5, 8-6)

_____

_____

_____

_____